Seer's Wisdom

Guidance for Spiritual Mastery

Almine

How to Flourish in All Areas of Your Life

Published by Spiritual Journeys LLC

First Edition June 2013

Copyright December 2012

MAB 998 Megatrust
By Almine
Spiritual Journeys LLC
P.O. Box 300
Newport, Oregon 97365

US toll-free phone: 1-877-522-5646

www.spiritualjourneys.com

All rights reserved. No part of this publication may be
reproduced without written permission of the publishers.

Cover Illustration – Dorian Dyer

Manufactured in the United States of America

ISBN 978-1-936926-52-7 Softcover

ISBN 978-1-936926-53-4 Adobe Reader

About the Author

Almine is a mystic, healer and teacher who has travelled for years through many countries, empowering thousands of individuals who are drawn to her comprehensible delivery of advanced metaphysical concepts. In the wake of her humility and selfless service, unspeakable miracles have followed.

In her life, made rich by the mystical and the holy, she has stood face-to-face with many of the ancient Masters of light, retaining full memory of the ancient holy languages in both written and spoken form.

Her teachings are centered on the idea that it is not only possible to live a life of mastery and love, but that it is the birthright of every human to attain such levels of perfection. Her journey has become one of learning to live in the physical, maintaining the delicate balance of remaining self-aware while being fully expanded.

"When we live in the moment, we live in the place of power, aligned with eternal time and the intent of the Infinite. Our will becomes blended with that of the Divine."

Almine

Introduction

(Excerpt from Almine's Journal dated January 2010)

"Long have I searched through space and time for the highest wisdom I could find. I thirsted for light to banish the night but a contradiction did I find. Light is one part of two separate poles — the brighter it shines the dimmer frequency grows.

Wisdom I did find, but it nourishes the mind when it is based on perception alone. Unless it is felt with the heart, love and compassion grow cold.

Like a ladder it is that reaches for the sky, but only so far can it go. Then one must fly into that which cannot be known. Beyond, indivisible life awaits. Wisdom leads one but to the unknowable's gates.

My thirst is quenched; my search is done, but the rapturous adventure has just begun — to discover the paradoxical embrace of the One."

Table of Contents

About the Author v
Introduction vii
Accessing Abundance 1
Dissolving Barriers to Abundance 37
Abundance in Relationship 103
Abundant Peace and Contentment 145
Manifesting an Abundant Environment 201
The Abundant Self 241
Abundance in Expression 303
Abundant Peace, Joy and Flourishing 359
Closing 417

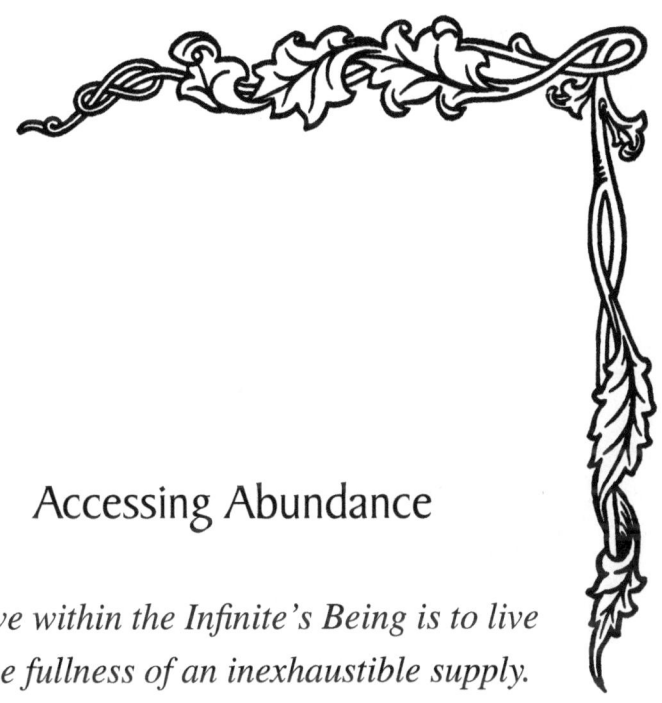

Accessing Abundance

To live within the Infinite's Being is to live in the fullness of an inexhaustible supply. Acknowledging the never-ending Source of abundance increases its accessibility.

The Earth is my cradle and the sky is my blanket. Wherever I go, I am home.

See yourself as part of the abundance of Creation. There are trillions of field flowers, grains of sand and stars. Your body too consists of abundant life. Let your affirmation be: "I am abundance".

Our being is our sustenance, and in our sovereignty, all our needs are supplied.

Seeing forms as unreal, we can become
the wolf or the rose or manifest more than
one form at will. It simply requires the firm
knowingness that they are not really there.

Live life as a work of art. Let an attitude of
graceful creativity enliven your financial affairs.

In acknowledging the oneness of man, all diverse
perspectives of the tribes of humanity become
ours and we become wealthy within.

Budgets block the torrential flow of abundance. Plan, but hold lightly to your plans, and expect abundant surprises.

Value illusion's role, for that which is not seen for the gifts it brings becomes distorted in its expression.

Hierarchies in life divide unless we realize that we are both the high and the low points of life: the high notes and low notes of the symphony.

To live beyond the boundaries of mortality, we
must live from the core of our being, as a presence
as vast as the cosmos having a human experience.

All-knowingness is not available through
mind but comes as the effortless and
spontaneous expression of the heart.

We promote abundance by being abundant
with ourselves. If we feel guilty about
having more than others, we deprive not
only ourselves, but them as well.

To masterfully create truth rather than
seek it, one must live an extraordinary
life beyond mortal boundaries.

Success and abundance are the only constants
in life. We either align ourselves with them
through surrender and trust, or cut ourselves
off from them through opposing life.

To desire to live abundantly is as natural
as the fish desiring the ocean. Money is
only a small part of abundance.

If you steadfastly hold before you the desires of your heart, life will present you with opportunities to fulfill them. Each day, watch carefully for unopened doors to knock on. Your heart will tell you which ones to step through when they open.

Embracing all as possible occurs when all definitions and expectations dissolve.

The true currency of an abundant life is elegance and grace born of self-respect. It is available to all.

When we bargain, we bar ourselves from
gain. The law of compensation decrees that
life too, will then short-change us.

One becomes captured by what one enslaves.

Abundance is living within your means with grace.
It has nothing to do with how much you earn.

The cosmic script is not predetermined. A planned future is a closed future. It is instead an endless array of joyous possibilities.

When our surrender eliminates our desires, we move into pure expression.

In living authentically from the heart, we come home to ourselves. In embracing the fullness of the moment, all is available to us now.

The level of consciousness determines the
level of truth that can be expressed.

Today's truth isn't tomorrow's truth; therefore,
hold on lightly to your beliefs. Truths
change as our perception changes.

Most who seek abundance instead focus on their
perceived lack, thereby strengthening it. See
yourself as part of the abundance of Creation.

Wherever diseases exist, a lack of harmonious
frequencies can be found in the body. Plants
can provide missing frequencies and therefore
restore health. The plant kingdom represents
the resource for adjusting frequency.

Acknowledgement of the Source of all abundance
as our self giving to our self increases the flow.

Grace and surrender are intricately connected.
The surrendered life unfolds with impeccable
timing and fluidity; yielding grace.

Accessing Abundance

If you desire flow to come to your life,
do not hoard. Donate that which you
do not use and throw away clutter.

A planned future is a closed future. Allow
yourself to dream and plan, but leave
enough room for life to surprise you.

When we notice the simple riches of nature, they
become our own. That within us, which they
reflect, is activated into fuller expression. We
cannot appreciate what we do not have within.

There is no limit to what can be known when
the mind is pure and the heart is innocent.

In the absence of thought all things are possible.
Thoughts arise from opposition to life. Let your
mantra therefore be: "I cease to oppose life".

See yourself as a steward of your possessions.
Treat them with respect, and repair rather
than replace them whenever practical.

I am the sovereign creator of my own reality. The ability to affect the quality of my journey begins with accepting full responsibility for the way in which Infinite Intent expresses through me.

We dwell in an ocean of abundance. We are limited only by our ability to recognize what is available.

In life's dealings, give the most you can and not the least. Otherwise you leave yourself in life's debt.

Meditation is the finger pointing at the moon. Reach for the moon and do not over-focus on the finger. Living with complete attention and surrendering to the moment accomplishes this.

The silent mind is the seat of genius
– the place of original thought where
effortless knowing takes place.

When we listen to our inner rhythms, our lives become fertile. Barrenness arises when we do not listen to the song of our heart.

Acknowledge with gratitude those who
serve you and life will support you.

Our being is our source of limitless supply.
We are heirs to the One Life's supply –
wealthy beyond our wildest dreams.

Some carry past hardships like stones in a
backpack up the mountain of life. Others use
them like wind beneath their wings.

A positive attitude begets increase. With a
surrendered embrace of life, the pushing
away of resources will cease. Centripetal
force, the result of an inclusive attitude, pulls
all towards you for a life of plenitude.

Money is the man-made life-blood of
society. It circulates, bringing back to
you that which you send out with it.

Asking for abundance while ignoring present
blessings closes one's ability to receive. Welcome
each new day the way a flower unfolds in the
sun, that the ability to receive may be yours.

Accessing Abundance

Principles of abundance are first learnt within the heart. When we give with joy, resources multiply.

At one with the flow of life, the need for sameness dissolves so that life can yield its surprises.

Living life as a spectator, observing its colorful pageantry, allows it to gracefully change through appreciation.

When we rise above the distortion of the matrix,
the breath-taking beauty of our fellow man will
be seen as the expression of our own being.
The Oneness of Life will then be obvious.

Abundance comes to one who lives in fullness.
Fullness comes from inclusive vision, gratefully
embracing the validity of every part of life.

When we neglect the feminine within
ourselves, our receptivity to abundance
becomes inactive and life becomes barren.

Living from the fully conscious life of wholesome values puts substance behind our endeavors. Soulless activity is hollow and cannot support abundance.

How do we reduce a burden of debt? Get professional assistance, and as in any long journey, do it one step at a time.

Inspiration arises when we uncover the perfection underlying appearances.

The drive for acquisition is the opposite of the
fullness of life abundant, for it presupposes a
lack. It is the little self that feels incomplete.
The large Self knows its own fullness.

Our being is an endless ocean of supply.
Our attitudes are its sluices. Through
inclusive living, the sluices open.

Gratitude opens the windows of heaven,
and abundance pours through. When we
send forth gratitude, the universe returns it
by giving us more to be grateful for.

Take moments in your day to assess your abundant resources: the joy of accomplishment, the love of a child. Then you will find you are wealthy indeed.

Since acceptance is the first step to change, seeing yourself as abundant in the moment is important to increasing abundant resources for the future. Take time each day to acknowledge your abundance with gratitude.

To think of money as a base currency is to forget that all that exists, is the One Life.

Contemplate the flawlessness of life and it will
reveal itself to you in endless synchronicities.

The ability to interpret feelings of rapture is
undeveloped in most and misinterpreted as
drowsiness. Cultivate feeling rapture by focusing
on that which evokes in you states of praise.

It is in refusing to accept the appearances
of limitation that we reveal the exquisite
perfection underlying all things. A miracle
is simply exploring this perfection.

Envision carefully what you wish to manifest.
Return to it several times a day, adding more
detail. See it as though it already exists.

Rather than focusing on what must be gone,
focus on that which must be expressed.

Live your life in fullness and everything
else will fall into place.

With all of man's striving to achieve and increase,
instead of abundance, he has increased his needs.
Free from desires and through daily gratitude,
man attracts success and the flow of plenitude.

Immovable emotional equanimity allows the
paceless unfolding of perfection to reveal itself.

Emotion, based on desire, implies lack or
scarcity. Deeply felt acknowledgement of
Oneness replaces the duality of emotion.

Spend money as a proxy. As you give a dollar to a person in need, give it by proxy, through intention, to all who are in need.

When you receive and hoard, you have become the tomb of abundance. When you receive and give, you are the womb of abundant flow.

All blessings-to-come begin by gratefully acknowledging present gifts. It decreases our supply when we focus on lack, instead of what we have.

Living in a rut reduces access to resources. A rut is only a rut because of unawareness.

Life is a collaboration between the One and the individuation. The little self may contribute its own unique perspective to enhance the quality of the journey.

Seeking abundance is a bottomless pit when it is defined as increase. We live in elegant sufficiency when we gratefully recognize we have all we need.

Reason predicts the future based on the past, thereby perpetuating the past. Only the heart can guide us through the uncharted territory of moments yet to come.

Life has been designed for mutual inspiration and encouragement. In living superficially, the inspiration and often the guidance offered by other life forms fall on infertile ground.

Knowing the Earth to be our source of supply, and our being to be our sustenance, we have established the foundation for prosperity.

We are in a society that lures us into debt as a way
of life. Resist this insanity as much as possible.
Save first, then buy. Your greatest asset is freedom.

Each day life presents doors for you to knock on.
Be alert for these multiple opportunities. Some
may open and some may not, but knock!

Would you bargain with your love, giving
only as little as you can? Then why would
you bargain and withhold money?

Give that you may get. One who generously assists wherever possible opens the sluices of cosmic supply.

Finding delight in the small things of life ripples out, creating larger expressions of delight. In this way, gratitude increases your joys.

What we appreciate, activates within us through resonance. What we are grateful for is increased and empowered. Appreciation and gratitude jointly heighten our capacity to receive.

As you wish for abundance, ask for the world, if
that is what you desire. If your desire is not met, no
matter – it was then a preference and not a need.

Look at the relationships and joys of your life
when you assess your abundance. No one is
impoverished who has access to nature and
the wealth of natural beauty it provides.

Paint life with a large brushstroke, but
do not neglect the details. So too, in
financial affairs where small leakages
can drain the reservoir of resources.

It is in knowing all within the Dream to be unreal that we transcend the make-believe world into the One Life of no beginning.

The flow of abundance is an illusion. We have always had access to all abundance.

The cost of excellence is discipline. The cost of mediocrity is disappointment.

Living in the unbounded expression of the
Song of Life is contagious. Through authentic
expression, the illusions come tumbling down.

Neither abundance nor poverty exists within the
Ocean of Life. When we know this, we are free.

Inclusively embracing life by finding all
that is praiseworthy, creates a centripedal
pull towards us of its resources. A positive
attitude thus creates abundance.

Contemplate with praise, the abundance of
the stars, the snowflakes, the field flowers.
For what you focus on, you become.

Through trust in our lives' infallibility and
our surrender to Infinite perfection, wondrous
events are immediately ours to seize.

We have become that which contains all
knowledge – it reveals itself by staying in
the moment within silence of the mind.

Like the flickering shards of light and shadow
cast on the wall by the fire in our hearth, many
beings march across the canvas of our eternal lives.
Allow them to come and go in fluid procession
that the adventure may be a pleasant one.

By staying in no-time, accomplishments are
numerous and limitless because effortless
knowing makes all possible in the now.

How do we draw on the limitless supply of
cosmic resources needed to overcome the
illusions of separation? By becoming the
ocean, the river, the sky and all that is.

A majestic quest requires the slowing of our pace to enable us to feel oneness. By becoming the eagle, our eyesight is restored: by being the ocean, our blood flows purely; by being the Earth, we stand in the strength of our Eternal Life.

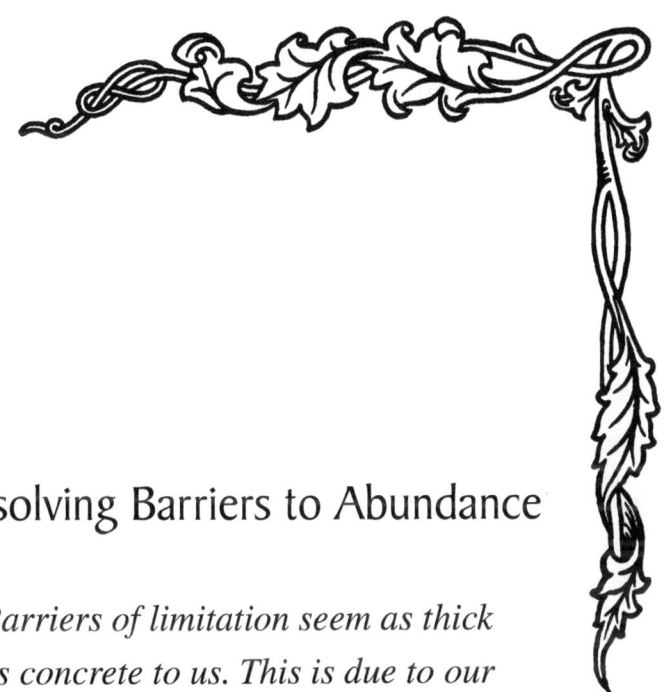

Dissolving Barriers to Abundance

Barriers of limitation seem as thick as concrete to us. This is due to our belief systems. When we see behind the appearance, they effortlessly dissolve.

As the One Life, we are all things. There is nothing to become. When we strive for more, we perpetuate impoverishment.

To look back and long for the highpoints of our lives is as unrealistic as a swimmer who wishes that the ocean would be one large crest of a wave.

Only balanced opposites can cancel one another out. This sets us free from space and time.

Confusion drains energy. When faced with
conflict or dilemma, choose to stay in stillness
until the answer to the matter reveals itself.

What we fight against multiplies. For in shattering
one mirror another stands revealed, reflecting
to us our imagined shortcomings. For, whether
we know it or not, perfection is all there is.

To wish that past events could be undone is
to wish to remove the burnishing fires that
forged the present luster of your life. A measure
of luster must then be forfeited also.

Spend only what you have so that you do not become the slave of dysfunctional needs.

When something cannot evolve into more refined expression, it deteriorates from stagnation.

Death and life are equally illusional. Beyond this polarity lies the transcendental existence of Oneness.

Let there be no regrets over right actions. Any action taken from authentic living benefits all involved, whether that is clear or not.

The vastness that intimidates is nothing more than the reflection of ourselves, yet we have seen it as that which guides our lives – the highest self.

Many petty squabbles are engineered by those who are afraid of relaxing into their vastness. They keep themselves from expansion by contracting their focus.

By cutting ourselves off from nature we lose sight of sound values and become steeped in blind materialism.

The soul has been called the higher self, but the hardships of our lives have been created by it as it tried to call the soul-force away from the body.

Self-importance, stemming from past accomplishments and pride of possessions, blocks the manifestation of an even greater future.

When money becomes the measuring
stick of our achievements, our desire for
wealth becomes an obsession.

The language of one who conveys facts is
dead. The words of one who speaks from
the heart are alive. This is because they
contain the full spectrum of tones.

In the core of every atom within every being, lies the
deep knowing that there is only the One Life. It is thus
prone to fight against that which seems to contradict
that knowing – the illusion that another being exists.

I relish the experience of unfolding existence.

The artificial creations of thought and
emotion disappear when we know that no
masculine or feminine has ever existed.
There is only indivisible androgyny.

Some acquire to live: others live to acquire. In both
instances, acquisition is a need rather than a joy.

Imagination sees what can be accomplished; fantasy dreams of having external solutions handed to us.

Fantasy promotes the misperception that change can occur without changing ourselves.

The tribe is one of the timing mechanisms of life. It tries to bind with conformity, keeping individuals in mediocrity. Those who wish to live in excellence must break free from the tribe.

Neediness creates agendas, which clouds clarity.

When we hold onto the situations of our life,
not allowing them to transform with grace,
we invite drastic change through death.

Embracing density as parts of ourselves
unlived, replaces stagnation with fluid
unfolding and graceful change.

When death is shunned and life is valued,
it persists as an instrument of change.

The heart is as much a tyrant as the mind, and is an unreliable source of information. Omni-sensory experience is a more reliable tool.

Man has revered the esoteric parts of his individuation as more pure than the physical, but one end of the stick is not holier than the other.

The fear of making mistakes, coupled with the realization that life is unknowable, causes man to cling to fragments of yesterday's truth. It is in self-trust as the One Being that we release our doubts.

Because life moves through us, we have no freedom of choice and hence no responsibility. The concept of freedom is like the hand saying to the body, "I want to be free".

The more we focus on a problem, the more we empower it. The same is true if we continually focus on a disease – we magnify it.

Structured programs of living, such as
social conditioning, act like viruses to life
and cause a dissonant reality. Observe
the origins of your actions to make sure
they do not arise from programming.

The soul and spirit are 'external' from the
individual and are artificial. It creates an enormous
drain on our resources to sustain such an illusion.

Many persuade by activating the subliminal
tones of the voice through conviction.
To prevent yourself from falling prey
to this, listen with detachment.

Thinking closes down access to limitless
faculties in the same way that belief systems trap
genius. In silence, all knowledge is ours.

Measure not accomplishment by that
which has been, lest it becomes the
limiting standard of tomorrow.

Yesterday's wisdom ended yesterday's
dream. It has very little application
to ending the dream of today.

The most virulent weed in the garden of
mastery is self-pity. Its twin, self-importance,
is not much less noxious. Preventing them
from taking root is a constant process.

If you feed the tiger it will take your hand
instead. It is not moral to pacify and indulge
the unreal: it is dysfunctional.

Heroism is the folly of thinking we have individual
choices, coupled with the arrogance of believing
we can improve life. Let us instead act as an
acknowledgement of the perfection of existence.

Inner conflict is the single most
important reason for aging.

Man refuses to acknowledge that which he is
addicted to, revering his own prison bars. One in
contraction places love on the throne of his life.
The expanded master reveres the detachment of one
who lives an impersonal life. Both are addictions.

When we see monetary resources as our security,
we deny that our being is our sustenance.

To measure our success by possessions is to be enslaved by the false values of social conditioning.

Effortless knowing does not need to pacify reason by proving itself. When the addictions of expanded awareness and ego-identification are removed, the graceful unfolding of life without the need to know remains.

As long as any programming exists in our lives, our feelings are unreliable sources for conveying the Infinite's unfoldment through us.

The belief that money has to be earned reduces the possibility that it can come from other sources.

From forgotten beginnings, belief systems grow, ensnaring our freedom. Examine carefully the origin of your actions lest the seeds of new ensnarements linger there.

To refuse to declare bankruptcy when extricating oneself from debt through other means is impossible; it is like the moth refusing to leave the spider's web on 'moral grounds'.

When the human soul feels alienated from Source, it seeks a situation that offers a sense of belonging – as in a tribe. The tribe however, stunts growth because it requires conformity. Solitude is the price of greatness.

There are those who seek to diminish your resources and achievements and those who try and profit from them. Neither believes they can achieve through their own efforts.

Like a wayward child that challenges the authority of the One Life's guidance, watch with benign humor the antics of mind. But like a wise parent, do not indulge them.

If you pacify the petty tyrants of your life for the sake of keeping peace, you will instead be promoting tyranny. In failing to learn the lessons they come to impart, you keep them on their treadmill of being unpleasant perception givers.

Aging and decay come through resistance to life, which causes the draining of resources by creating a centrifugal force around the body.

Some feel guilt at having too much and others at having too little. Guilt clogs the arteries of supply.

Vigorously uproot belief systems that indoctrinate
with perceived status symbols and fabricated needs.

The weight of comparisons will impede us
as we dance with the abundance of life.

Considering the worth of the recipient of our gifts
is to close the conduits of our own supply, for
to deny another's worth is to deny our self.

Envying others their life of ease, is to mistake complacency for comfort. Comfort comes from the deep satisfaction growth brings.

Remembering either good deeds or injuries creates a burden of illusion. We are but the One Life in expression, giving to ourselves.

Think of form as a transient snow flurry in the wind – formless yet forming, that we might escape the blinding illusion of its unyielding solidness.

Allowing those who unsuccessfully manage their
own lives, to manage part of ours, is as foolish
as the patient trying to treat the physician.

Resistance to life is a centrifugal force
pushing bounty away as resources
spin outwards within our space.

When we deplete our physical resources, our
abundance dwindles as well. Fatigue comes from
resistance to life. Fatigue indicates that impeccability
of vision is required, not more rest, for we can
rest while we work and work while we rest.

Do not give strength to the illusion of past losses.
In the flawlessness of life, no loss can occur that is
not fully compensated. In pure beingness, where no
opposites exist, neither loss nor compensation is real.

Feeling needed by others feeds self-importance.
This applies even to subtle needs, such as affection.

Only in duality do problems exist. A problem only
exists because its solution is already there, for each
is defined by its opposite. When we live in the One
Life, neither problems nor solutions have any reality.

Money represents crystallized power.
If you spend it with guilt, the presence
of guilt in your life is empowered.

When we want our lives to change, while
refusing to let go of the old, the pathways
of abundance are blocked. Letting go with
grace ensures a more abundant life.

Discernment is born of the heart. Judgment
is of the mind. The mind, unlike the
heart, can only draw its conclusions
from face value. This is judgment.

Man desperately clings to his familiar obsessions, preferring them over the unsteady ground of freedom. When temporarily relieved of them, he interprets their absence as an emergency, feeling empty and lost. As a result, he hastens to reach yet again for his prison bars.

Do not seek to understand nor be understood, but rather dance with the contradiction of beingness, clothed boldly in the cloak of unknowingness.

There is no growth needed, but neither can there be stagnation. Stagnation must yield to the exuberant gushing forth of the One Life.

Ruthlessly eliminate focusing on what is not how we want it to be – this only increases the illusion of lack.

Focusing on lack instead of supply promotes depletion. All blessings come through gratefully acknowledging present gifts.

When we cut ourselves off from nature, we lose sight of sound values and become steeped in blind materialism.

Conviction does not equate with accuracy. Yet many
follow blindly because they are deluded into thinking
they can know when life is essentially unknowable.

Seeing the body as having many different parts
and organs, an inside and an outside, is but
an illusional program imposed by mind in an
attempt to label the incomprehensible.

By reducing acquisition, appreciation is found for
what we have. Always looking beyond the horizon
leaves the surrounding landscape unappreciated.

The shadows in our lives are nothing more
than the tricks we play on ourselves to
express previously unyielded potential.

Wherever it is imagined that more than one
being exists, an anomaly has been conjured
up. Life does not support an anomaly but
opposes it. Hence conflict forms.

The past becomes a ball and chain
if we drag it into the future.

Massive industries and institutions are built
to feed on the achievements and misfortunes
of others. Surround yourself with those who
believe in their own accomplishments.

Celebrate your successes and accomplishments,
but do not take them seriously. Neither
success nor failure can be ours when
there is only One Life expressing.

Memory is not a friend, it is a foe. It is
in releasing memory that all that can
be known becomes accessible.

The twin flaws of boredom and uncouthness
alike find their origin in common ground - lack
of awareness of the infinite worth of all life.

Many programs designed by mind, such
as religion, have reduced the value of
the body. These are tools to control the
indescribable wonder of the body.

Rejecting any part of ourselves creates a barrier
that excludes the infinite resources of the One Life.

The illusion of pain being inflicted by others
or that life misinterprets us, comes from our
illusory belief systems. But they too are unreal –
the ocean is always whole by nature.

Responsibility can be like an identity carried
like a heavy burden or a badge. We can
become identified as someone who can be
counted on. All identity traps awareness.

There is a fear that the One Life's vastness
is boring. But it needs to be experienced
with more than our illusory perception for
the indescribable glory to reveal itself.

I am free from the illusory realities of opposites.

Conformity does not make the soul feel
at home, but rather causes it to withdraw
in pain. This strengthens materialism.

The illusion of there being wisdom implies
that the indefinable can be defined, and that
there are static points in infinite unfolding.

Addiction arises from self-abandonment. Mind
abandons its inner knowingness by trying to
understand through answers from without.

Do not lend empowerment through attention
to financial doomsday predictions. Prepare
for the worst and expect the best.

Thought keeps the past in place, like calcifications
that constrict the present. Only by replacing thought
with effortless knowing do they dissolve.

Where families have been supported by
large debt structures, a necessary economic
readjustment is to be expected. Substance
must replace such hollowness. Forced change
may not become necessary if, instead, we
alter our lifestyles with dignity and grace.

To regret the loss of resources is to deny
that we are the creators of our lives and
can create as much abundance again.

The illusion of 'correct' and 'incorrect' implies
that anything contrary to the real can exist.

When we do not live with acknowledgement of the interconnectedness of life, the fragmentation of the self causes the madness of egocentricity.

Compassion embraces another's growth.

Enabling others to view you as their line of credit is to promote disempowerment and a misplaced sense of entitlement.

The desire for the comfort of structure is the remnant of relying on the false promises of mind.

Anger and rage are like destructive fires that erupt when you cannot see that you create your own life.

It is only when we deny part of existence to be, that it becomes adversity.

Many value knowledge and seek it above all else. But what is knowledge but the static perception of yesterday's unfolding life?

Do not support the worldview of those who seek the most they can get, that you may not be encumbered by parasitic ties.

Beauty seen with the eyes is the illusory beauty of form that, like the clay pot, delights today and fragments tomorrow.

Those who take in greed deplete not only
themselves, but others as well.

Acknowledge that that which causes
opposition and heartache, is merely ourselves
getting in the way of the inexorable
perfection unfolding through our lives.

When we look back, the past comes alive in the
present. When we look forward, we create a future
with only the possibilities of the moment and
without the contribution of moments yet to come.

Taking resources for granted depletes them. All things dwindle in the face of ingratitude.

The fear of cataclysmic Earth changes stems from our thinking either we can manifest them or that we are powerless to prevent them.

Mercy comes from guilt. Guilt comes from judgment and judgment comes from an inability to see that anything that exists serves a purpose or it would not be there.

Regrets come when we believe we have had success and failures. As a part of the One Life's Dream, life simply flowed through us.

To live asleep is to think life is duty. To awaken is to find that life is beauty. Many parents drive their children to acquire skill sets and achievements, forgetting to teach them how to be happy.

Life's song becomes discordant when we focus on illusion, the unsung notes of life. Our focus makes them change from potential sound to actual inharmonious tone.

Not only is debt a form of enslavement, but it also creates the unwholesome situation where we do not own the food we eat or the clothes we wear – the bank does.

Critical thinking without creative thinking is destructive. Creative thinking without critical thinking perpetuates mediocrity. The heart bypasses both through effortless knowing.

The societal structure has been a surrogate parent. The fear of society falling apart is the fear of being abandoned by a parent.

To fulfill your heart's desires before those
of someone else, allows us to give to
others from a position of wholeness.

Do not try and 'fix' your shortcomings. They are
not there by accident. They are the indicators
of areas where life is not fully lived or insight
has not been gained from experiences.

All addictions are the result of self-abandonment.
The addiction to spending is no different. Balanced
spending comes from balanced living.

Approaching food with the desire to gain its nutrition is to taint it with an agenda. Instead, share the abundance of its life-force by savoring it with appreciation.

Greed is born from seeing resources as limited, which in turn comes from living a life of boundaries.

As spider webs catch a moth, so do programs catch the human soul. Free yourself from them with vigor.

All realities have merged into one, as have mind and feeling. It requires allowing ourselves to see and dissolve old obsolete boundaries.

Guilt over incurred debt blocks future flow. Any beneficial change requires acceptance of the present.

A lower level of existence explores life by examining ways that life is not. A higher life explores the beauty and purity of what is.

When our existence is consumed with duty, the
heart feels deprived and life becomes impoverished.
No amount of money can compensate for that.

Do not hang back from knocking on doors before
you because you do not know whether you would
want to enter. Wonderful surprises may lie beyond.

Life cannot imprison us where we do not
wish to be or bind us when we wish to be
free. It is only in the self-imagined prisons
of our lives that suffering is created.

The only government that can possibly exist is the governing of the One Life. All else is the unreal attempting to govern that which is also unreal.

Because of the false claim of the body to be real, we feel self-pity through comparison.

No opposites exist within the One Life.
As long as a life of opposites is lived,
we cannot know our Oneness.

The fear of being out of control creates the illusion that there is the need to be grounded. We are out of control because our physical lives are guided by the Infinite Life. If we are meant to fly, we will.

Failure is not lack of success:
it is being afraid to try.

Mind has been the worst offender in creating illusion, but heart's attachments have been keeping it in place.

Within the matrix of opposites – the imaginary space of duality – others are mirror images of ourselves and mirrors reflect distortion. Within the matrix, feeling oneness with distortion becomes difficult unless we realize that behind the obvious appearances lies the perfection of eternity.

Judge not a slow pace as more praiseworthy than a fast one. In timelessness, the concept of pace does not exist.

A life of unyielded insights is shallow, creating the internal dialogue of the mind that traps one in the world of appearances.

The more we strive for enlightenment, the stronger the pull to keep us down. Levitation must be balanced by gravitation. Only in changeless change is there no polarity.

Many say they seek truth, but instead seek to confirm already-held belief systems. Their prison bars of belief thus grow thicker and thicker.

Promises contain within them a lie. When life and all beings are renewed in each eternal moment, it is untrue to promise an outcome or even our intent to create an outcome.

When we approach anything with the question of
"What is the most I can get?", scarcity arises.
Let us approach food with appreciation
rather than a need for nutrition.

Self-pity creates a downward spiral in our
circumstances, since what we focus on increases.

Ingratitude stems from lack of awareness and
the failure to see the multiple miracles unfolding
around us. Mind demands the sensational,
but the heart embraces the subtle.

Do not let your work dictate the pace of your life. Dedicate time slots in which you respond to its demands. In this way, it does not become the master and you the slave.

When we try and fix life, we are resisting life, which judges and divides. Acknowledging wholeness uplifts.

The only true tragedy is a fruitless life. Failing to gain the insights of experience squanders life and invites unpleasant lessons.

Believe in nothing, for only then can
you freely and effortlessly know.

The more we focus on one thing to the exclusion
of others, the more limited life becomes.
To focus on any part of life is to attempt to
hold a gushing fountain in a bucket.

Life's burdens consist of unyielded
insights. We either die to our old way of
being each day through deep, meaningful
living or we invite death to relieve us.

As conduits for the flow of Infinite
resources, we should view ourselves
as custodians rather than owners.

The principle of compensation decrees that
anything worthy of life that is denied the right
to exist, receives increased virility. That which
you oppose is therefore strengthened.

Power and light are inseparably connected.
To seek light, while with false humility
shunning power, is a contradiction.

When previous financial systems fail us,
looking for solutions within those systems
seldom works. Think outside the box.

The soul justifies its excesses and indulgences through
self-pity. Uproot self-pity ruthlessly as it obscures truth.

Accepting the unacceptable is not saintly;
it is dysfunctional. It is your sacred duty
to safeguard the divine heritage you have
received from the Infinite's hand.

Self-pity looks outside itself to be rescued.
Self-responsibility finds a solution within.

Presenting yourself as less than who you really are, in order to gain the acceptance of others, keeps both you and them on the treadmill of mediocrity.

Do not use money as a substitute to giving of yourself as it causes an imbalance that creates lack for you and others.

Personal labels can be assumed to aid in manifesting intent. They only obscure truth when we believe them to be all that we are.

Opposition is no longer the way of growth, nor is growth required. Hardships are no longer needed as we move into a deathless society.

That which is always new can never be known. It is futile to strive to understand when we live in the unknowable.

What androgyny truly is, is the fullest
expression of both feminine and masculine,
thus blending into one glorious whole.

In pure androgyny and the knowing of our indivisibility
from the One, eternal timelessness is ours.

From times of pressure come new births.
From the contrast of expression comes the
artistry of life's dance. Embrace it all.

Truth masquerades as something desirable.
It is nothing more than a futile attempt to
capture the insight that the moment brings.

Form becomes more and more solid the more
you live with programs, worldviews, belief
systems, personal identity and personal history.

Let us stop creating reality from what has been.

Anything that can be defined can be taken away. Anything that is in identity can be lost.

The ultimate purpose of failure is to steer us in the way of success; it is nothing more than a way-shower of life's course.

Self-control is still a desire to control life. In the matrix, it is part of mastery. In oneness, beyond duality, it serves no purpose.

Belief systems are distorted light, and
therefore, a form of disease.

Many seek to know the laws of existence that
they might influence its course. True mastery
lies in the surrender to its spontaneity.

Stagnation of resources comes from ruts. Let the
adventure of life unfold anew in your life daily.

Mind and emotions create mediocre drama. The One Life lives the greatest adventure of all.

In the pressure of opposition, let us see the Infinite learning about Itself by feeling the contours of Its face. In conflict, let us know Its Self-embrace.

Courage is only needed to override the objections of the mind. When the mind is still, right action is automatic.

The true battle of a light promoter is against illusion. Every encounter with opposition is a chance to pierce the illusion and find the hidden perception.

The tension produced by resistance to life obstructs the pure messages of the Infinite and of the majestic being man is meant to be. Living in timelessness reveals them.

Because of the tendency to be overwhelmed by our vastness, we create a personal history as a reference point of identity. Identity, as a trap, must be shed to be a truly free cosmic being and inheritor of limitless power.

Man as the densest being has the greatest latent
power within in order to sustain such density.
By living in expanded awareness, we become
less dense and the power becomes available.

In duality, the answers and the questions never cease and
every question answered, begets another yet to be solved.

We give false credit to illusion as being
growth-promoting. When we forget our light,
illusion reminds us of its existence.

There is nothing to accomplish or achieve.
The One Life moves through us in abundant
expression and all we need to do is allow.

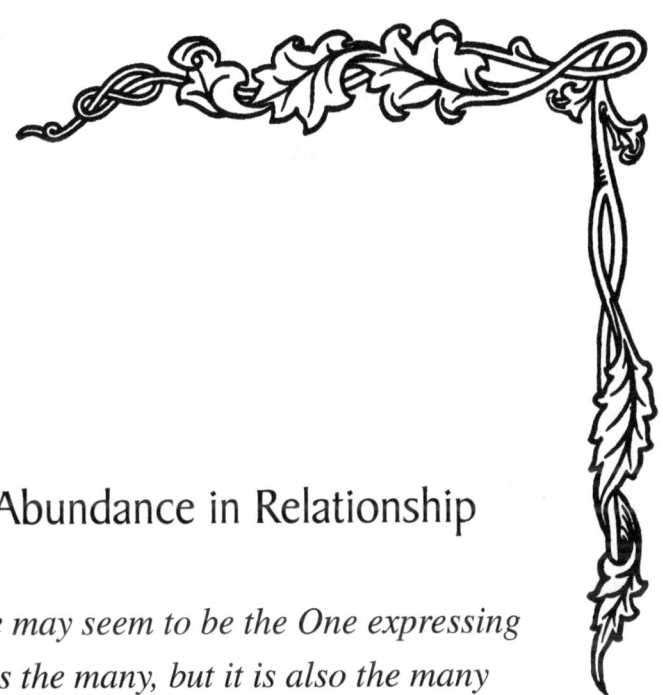

Abundance in Relationship

Life may seem to be the One expressing as the many, but it is also the many expressing as the One. Each is all that is, and relationships therefore do not exist; they are roles we play to illustrate the infinite variety of expression within the One.

Acknowledgement of another's Divine Oneness creates the dissolving of his personal matrix, effortlessly elevating him into the One Life.

Life is indivisible oneness. A perceived relationship is but me examining myself.

Relationships are like a river – their dynamics shift. Appraising them regularly is essential for the wellbeing of all.

When others cannot hear our words because of
their lower consciousness, the greatest gift we
can give them is the accepting compassion of
our tone. Then, what is said is immaterial.

It is in weathering the storms of relationship
that the ability to love deepens – for it is there
we find and heal our shortcomings.

Speech without authenticity empowers the
masculine, separative qualities of life. Speaking
from the heart promotes inclusivity.

What we love, we create a relationship with.
What we create a relationship with will ultimately
bind us. Embracing another in the agenda-
less freedom of knowing ourselves to be all
things is the love of divinity expressed.

In seeing the poverty of another, we are
observing an impoverished part of ourselves.
Fix within what is imperfect without.

For total Oneness to exist, all beings must be
androgynous, their masculinity and femininity
blended into one in a perfect harmonious union.

All life has equal value. There is no lesser or higher standard of conduct if we realize that our choices are guided by the One Life.

We nurture the illusions that we teach and advise others, thinking that we know what is best for them. Their past is illusory and cannot help us determine the newness of their moment.

Learning to love without pain and live without agenda is humanity's greatest challenge.

Adversity can teach us and our family more
than many years of prosperity, but only if we
enthusiastically pick up the gauntlet.

No life is unimportant. No strand can
be removed from the spider web of life
without disturbing its perfection.

Interact sparingly with the games of men;
interact deeply with the moment.

We think we dwell in the same reality as everyone else, but each dwells in a separate reality of his own making, shaped by thoughts and feelings like rushing waters carving the canyon walls.

Surround yourself with those who, like you, seek to give the most possible so that you are supported by winners.

Man has lived from madness, creating an artificial reality. It is not compassionate to indulge folly and participate in the madness, but rather to usher in a higher truth by example.

When loved ones succumb to death, we may not be able to communicate between realms but we can within the Oneness of our Being. Death cannot separate that.

The fear of being rejected because others see us as different does not acknowledge the fact that within the One Life, there is no sameness – only Oneness.

Other than Divine Compassion, all types of love are the sub-creations of man. Human love binds; Divine Compassion sets all potential free.

To see poverty in another is to disacknowledge the
cosmic compensation for any seeming loss.

Relationship creates space, the way enamored lovers
carve their hearts upon a tree. Within the creation of such
an illusion lies the seeds of its own demise, for the drain
of resources to sustain illusion must ultimately deplete all
involved. Only in the freedom of oneness can all flourish.

There is no possibility of injuring another or
of letting them down. We are the One and
design all experience from the One Life.

Exclusive love cannot live in the
absence of value judgment.

Interaction with others must come from delighted
exploration and not from expectations, habits or duty.

We think we are shaped by the experiences
from our past, but in truth, we are only
shaped by our belief in them.

Any relationship is an illusion within the
One Life – even the inner relationship
of the observer and the observed.

Seek not to bring contentment to others,
for in doing so you will lose your own.

The illusional game of relationship becomes
enjoyable when we cut the ties of expectation.

Frugality has nothing to do with how much
we spend, but in how impeccably we refuse to
squander energy through playing dysfunctional
games with others and through resisting life.

Polarity persists where hierarchies exist. No-thing
can be more important than another when they are
opposites. Two sides of one coin are equally valuable.

Opposition must be gratefully acknowledged
as the tool of individuation. It is that which has
enabled the joyful dance of relationship.

All beings play parts to form the kaleidoscope of
changing life within the One Being. All are therefore
innocent participants in the joyous pageantry of existence.

We love others' personalities created from the illusions
of life, instead of experiencing the divine compassion of
the formlessness of our beings in an endless embrace.

To free ourselves from the ties of relationship
requires times of solitude, for only then do
we discover the fullness of ourselves.

Do not envy another's journey, for only the one you are on can lead you to the glory of victory over illusion.

Change through critical mass is obsolete in that it determines evolution through quantity. It is in the quality of the One Life that all changes.

The seeming creation of beings of illusion is like the soul-less chairs we sit on: an illusory sub-creation of man.

Over-valuing another's level of awareness
is as detrimental as under-valuing it.

Never think you can know another's truth from your
vantage point. You can only learn it from them.

You are not separate from another. Both are an
inter-related and merged field. Appearing separate
is simply due to a peculiarity of vision.

In interacting with those asleep in lower consciousness, let us meet in the half-light of awakening. To shower the one who will not hear, with higher truth will only prolong his sleep through blinding his vision with the brightness of our light.

The only way relationship can truly be sublimated is by knowing we reside as one within the fullness of life.

Nothing can give nor receive. There is no passivity or pro-activity, nor masculinity and femininity. Life is experienced equally by all.

Do not expect loyalty nor give loyalty. The only
loyalty anyone of high consciousness can have is
to the impeccable expression of authenticity.

The presence of divinity at the heart of all individuations
connects us all. When one note on the piano resonates,
all do. In this way, the one affects the many.

Treating ourselves with abundant care and
nurturing is the first step to an abundant life.

All individuals are trustworthy because
they have no volition of their own – the
One Life is unfolding through them.

One thing can seem to temporarily negate another
only when it enlarges itself at the expense of
the other and if it is its polar opposite.

To consider the recipient's worth when giving
is to close the sluices of our supply, for to deny
another's worth is to deny ourselves.

Relationships based on duality that seem to last
are based on a pact of stagnant dysfunctionality.
Only in knowing ourselves to be the other in
total Oneness can there be eternal newness.

Because our light is brighter than others does not mean
that they may not yet surpass our brightness. Only the
Choreographer spontaneously delegates the parts.

Much of what we wish to teach our children
we ourselves do not know. Throughout the
generations, dogma has replaced the skillful art
of living impeccably. Let us learn together…

Self-reflection obstructs the purity of spontaneous living by creating self-relationship.

Consideration for others allows all to express at their own level of awakening. For the dream is no more real than the awakening. As you allow them theirs, so life is best served when you maintain yours through sparing interaction.

The artificial construct of relationship must, by nature, become a battleground. All opposite poles fight for survival.

When brought into a higher functionality,
opposite poles inspire one another,
rather than opposing one another.

The Inner Child has been weighted down by
memories the masculine stored in the magnetic
because he was unable to interpret them. The roles
must reverse; he receives the question and the
feminine's greater inclusiveness must interpret.

Family life must support all individuals
equally, rather than supporting the tribe.

To suffer because of the hardship of others is to imply that imperfection exists – that the One Life cannot support Itself in a benign way.

Power is the result of not having relationship. Relationship keeps static form in place.

By proclaiming illusion to have no hold over you because it does not exist, is to have an illusory relationship with a shadow.

Tolerance and respect for others does not mean you should allow disrespect of the sacred space in which you live and work.

Comparisons will either make us feel poor because we have less, or guilty because we think we have more. Each one has manifested their life in divine perfection. Let us honor this.

Propriety is nothing more than another's values censoring our actions. Let freedom from concern over others' judgments and opinions be a conscious decision.

Feelings are not pure as long as there is identity. The heart cannot open fully within the confines of identity.

One of the greatest weights mankind has carried is the concept of comparisons. This creates the striving of competitiveness.

In acknowledging the perfection behind appearances, blameless interaction takes place.

The two greatest obsessions are the need to know and the presence of emotions. Both create the illusion of relationship, as emotions are based on desire for an external source of fulfillment, and the need to know is based on the desire to control external circumstances.

Comparisons and self-reflection create polarity. In turn, polarity creates the shadow of adversity.

When we allow others to take from us and pillage our lives, our time and our resources, we keep them from accomplishing on their own.

The feminine is incomprehensible and the
masculine cannot understand nor fix her.
When he expresses fully, he too, becomes the
incomprehensible expression of divinity.

We can never be lost within the vastness of
life. What we are encountering is our self.

Living within appropriateness and propriety is living
within an illusion-based personal matrix, created by
others for the sake of control through conformity.

The most powerful manipulators are those who choose to appear helpless and inept. The ones who fall into their traps are those with a need to save.

No approval from others can ever be valid, for they cannot understand the unique perspectives and contributions of our lives.

There can be no disagreements, just the elevating of self to a new level. There is only Oneness.

Each being is a series of gateways to the magical realms beyond, yet inter-locking with ours.

Nurturing of others must occur from our largest awareness, as a consciousness superimposed over all that is, to prevent being trapped by social protocol.

The illusion of relationship is a game for the sake of delight. Money is a man-made game within a game, and should also be for delight.

The respect given by others is of little value unless they have learnt to see behind face values – a skill most never achieve. Otherwise, not being based on true value, that respect can easily be withdrawn.

Because of co-dependence, old doors stay open when they should be closed. New doors will not open until the old ones are shut.

Since all are obeying the song of the One Life, all are expressing impeccably.

One of the problems of relationship is that we romanticize un-wholeness and dysfunctionality.

In the timeless companionship of true beingness, we play on the stage of form. We know that there is nothing to improve – perfection is complete.

To have relationship not founded in Oneness is to abandon the self because it implies separation. Separation denies the source of our being.

When the inner child is not properly parented,
we seek uniformity through relationships, even
when other areas of our life are in mastery.

True listening takes place in the absence of
thought. Only then can you enter into the
experience of another's world. To truly listen to
someone is to assimilate a new perspective.

Living the One Life is the greatest
contribution we can make to the whole.

One cannot understand a being as vast as
the cosmos having a human experience:
to try would be arrogant disrespect.

Each family member has a psychological poverty
consciousness trigger. For example, the housewife may
need a supply of canned food to feel abundant. As far
as possible, honor these triggers for your family.

To avoid being caught in the social games
of others, the nurturing of them must
be done from the expanded self.

Separation has brought comfort to the parts of Creation developing at different speeds. Recognize this, for separation to yield to Oneness.

Many feel guilt because they have more, while others feel guilt because they have less. There will always be alternating areas within beingness where certain resources are more emphasized. Equalization produces mediocrity.

The cohesive force of the cosmos is relationship. Only the most profane dare to enter the temple of learning through relationship with anything other than profound reverence.

Lasting friendships must inspire mutual growth if they are to be life-enhancing. The only other way they could last is through conformity – the death knell of greatness.

No timing mechanism is needed when all become One. When all can communicate, fully integrated purpose will come.

Living on the treadmill of polar opposites reveals that opposites travel in pairs. Within one, the other can be found; within life, decay abounds. In recognizing the value of both, we can transcend them.

If you give to another, consider the extent of his need.
He may need a skill, or to be put in touch with an agency
or a month's rent. Next, consider your capacity to give.

Only in the complete silence of the mind can you
enter into the empathic understanding of another.

The barometer of the strength of a relationship
is how well problems can jointly be solved.
Rage-filled outbursts come from those who
believe they have no other way to be heard.

The highest form of compassion is to surround yourself with those who inspire joy and to shun those who do not. Because opposite frequency attracts, your joy will automatically be attracted to the most joyless place on earth.

In acknowledging the wholeness of the incorruptible part of another, we assist that being in letting go of its addiction to the Dream.

The difference between creations of greatness and those of lesser consciousness is the height at which they fly and the vistas that they see.

We can see in others either chaos or
Oneness. Whatever we choose to see, we
do not need to engage but to envelop.

Tenderly treat others, for they are as you make
them. You are the dreamer of your dream.

Do not suppose that because others listen in earnest
that they hear you. True listening can only take
place in the absence of the dialogue of the mind.

Those who 'love' you while they are in ego-consciousness cannot actually feel love for you, because from such contracted vision they cannot see you. Truly seeing you must acknowledge your limitless divinity. In the absence of this, only attachment can occur.

That which we don't express of ourselves, we fall in love with in others.

We have awakened to our true heritage to find we are all that is. As such we are at all times directly in touch with all life. To love one more than another is to love an arm more than a leg. They may serve different purposes, but are all us.

Let genuine words of praise flow from your
mouth, for in seeing the praiseworthy in another
we have just found it in ourselves. One can only
recognize without, that which is within.

Because all are created from the body of the
Infinite, all are by nature, flawless. All conduct is
therefore simply the song of life singing to itself.

Fly where your heart takes you, inspired
and unafraid. He who waits for the approval
of others has clipped his own wings.

We awakened to our Oneness, only to find
the joy of relationship made it desirable to
pretend we were separate yet again.

Relationship brings pain, finding
oneself in another brings rapture.

Only when it is remembered that the masculine
and feminine have never really been separated,
does one live beyond the contradiction.

Let each encounter be an unwritten book, approached
with the willingness to be pleasantly surprised.

Character is formed one choice at a time. However,
two ingredients always present are firmness
with oneself and gentleness with others.

Abundant Peace and Contentment

*Lie back in the peaceful arms of
the One Life. Even if the worst you
fear comes about, the loving
arms of the Infinite will lift you
up and over such hardships.*

We are the flute and the music. The
music that we allow to express through
us is the song of the One Life.

All reveals itself through the silent surrender of our being.

There cannot be conflict or solutions, but rather creative
flow. It is the fallen tree that alters the river's course
and provides the spontaneous change in its shape.

In looking at life, we may think that wrong choices
were made, but since we never really made
them of our own volition, it is impossible.

The boundless resources of the One Life are
ours and because our body is an illusion,
our depletion of it is imagined.

My existence is an androgynous expression
of the exquisite grace of the One Life.

Nothing new can ever exist, except for the newness of our response to it. We have assumed forgetfulness in order to respond with surprise.

Let go of logic first, then comes the new day.

There is nothing to learn and everything to enjoy. Created life was formed for the self-delight of the One Life.

In the enthusiasm for the adventure of self-discovery do we find our hopes fulfilled.

Experiences are neutral since there is neither good nor bad. This realization allows us to simply enjoy life spontaneously.

In living in devotion to the Song of the One Life coursing through our lives, we are living in service to all.

No need to reach without to strive,
when all within you is alive.

We are not needed by the Infinite to help shape life,
but rather given the opportunity to share in the joy.

The purity of my essence precedes me. Waves of creative
unfolding flow through me in everlasting rapture.

At no time does life require that we understand it. The One Life knows all and from our small perspective, it is incomprehensible.

Karmic repercussions for debt cannot exist, since there is no time and within the One Life, debt is an illusion.

We think we procrastinate, but the cosmos unfolds with immaculate timing. We are always exactly on time.

Enlightenment is a journey, not a camp.
There is never a point of arrival. Let the
journey therefore be a grand adventure.

The challenges we embrace don't have to be painful.
As we become more adept at seeing behind the
appearances, we can learn the lessons effortlessly.

Like a child trying to catch a cloud, every attempt
of ours to find a flaw in the unfolding of life must
be vanquished by the patient passage of time.
There is neither imperfection nor perfection
– just the inexorable revelation of the endless
majesty of the Infinite in expression.

There is no possibility of missing opportunities.
If they are part of the choreography of the One
Life, we shall most certainly choose them.

Swim in the ocean of abundance
and you shall never want.

Deeply felt acknowledgement of Oneness is the
appreciation of the ever-renewing Self as all that is.

Through surrendered trust, I am completely fluid.

Seek not meaning, for it retains that which has become meaningless. Perception without conclusion brings clarity.

Living in full surrender to the Oneness of our being, we live in the full support of the Infinite Embrace.

I live in Infinite unfolding grace.

The greatest illusion of all is the division
between that which is and that which is not.
Beyond such duality lies Oneness.

We are not responsible for carrying life, instead
it is cradling us in a cherished embrace.

Joy seeks company. Finding the sources of joy
and delight in our day multiplies them.

There are no flawed choices. There is only the journey
of perfection along which we are tenderly guided.

Oneness experiences itself through multiplicity, entrained
to the symphony of the unfolding of the One Life.

Your being is limitless; claim its abundant majesty.

Let us release the responsibilities of the Dream that we may relax into memory-less spontaneity.

Eliminating mind that judges and divides requires complete surrender to life. From resistance arise thoughts that confine, creating ties that bind.

In the grateful acknowledgment of joyous gifts,
unprecedented miraculous encounters take place.

Humility means we stand in silence before the wonder
of our being and allow it to reveal everything to us.

Disease as a reality does not exist. Healing can come
in an instant when the language of the ailment is
understood as an indicator of dysfunction in your life.

Life cannot take away without compensating
us. A hole cannot be made in the ocean.
Watch for new areas of abundance.

The destiny of every life form is to explore the unknown.
A lower level of life explores it by examining unknown
ways that life is not. A higher life explores unknown
ways to express the beauty and purity of what is.

In contented surrender and peace, our
joyful expectations are surpassed.

We are on a path that has no point of arrival because
there is no destination. There is only the journey.

Nothing is unknown to the Infinite because we
dwell within its Being. The amount we can know
is limited only by our willingness to receive.

Prayer is the One Voice expressing through
our Eternal Being in pure harmony.

There is no predictability to the spontaneous unfoldment of the One Life. Prophecy cannot exist.

Mother Earth is more than an ally; she is intimately connected with us through the heart.

Like the wind lifting the autumn leaves into the air, the winds of seeming adversity are our allies. It is an opportunity to stir from our complacency, and in a surrendered embrace of life's adventure, allowing the unexpected to invigorate our existence.

The unfoldment of the One Life is
unstoppable. No obstruction is possible.

Fear not your tears more than your laughter, for they carve the hallows of the soul with which to contain your joys, the same way that light is defined by shadow.

We must learn to trust in ourselves and know that we are connected to the Source that breathed life into us – the I Am that I Am. Then we can lie back in the arms of Spirit and simply be, having faith that we will be taken care of.

Fullness is mine by embracing
unfolding life in wonderment.

No matter your choices of paths to traverse, the journey since birth that you travel on Earth, all roads lead up the mountain of timelessness and into the arms of eternity.

The body is a fluid vehicle of a being as vast as
the cosmos, having a human experience.

Confusion is but a momentary game we play of hide and seek. If we open our eyes we see that all knowledge pertaining to the moment is ours.

When the inner and outer meet, you become a field. They blend as one.

Denying the value of another's unconsciousness is like expecting the music to improve by playing all notes at once.

Man feels insignificant when compared to the vastness of the cosmos. But because space does not exist, size is nothing to the Infinite and every portion is the whole.

The nature of life is spontaneous unfoldment. By allowing it to flow through us, fluidly changing direction as needed, we enter into mastery.

Nothing can be defined nor measured. Living from the One Life through form, our presence cancels out such illusions.

True peace is my constant companion
through embracing unknown change.

My experience of life is ever-rejuvenated.

In the rippling of a deed through the
interconnectedness of life, no act remains small.

Density is the note that is not played, as it awaits
its turn to add to the exquisite symphony of life.

I embrace the unknowable unfolding of existence.

Not only do the silent spaces of our life provide
the guidance for authentic expression, but
they also give the deep nourishing soil for
our exponential insights to take root.

The definition of a spiritual life is to see behind appearances. This is the first step in becoming free from the tyranny of form – which is mastery.

In the place of no opposites, life stills and enters timelessness. Aging ceases and decay has no hold.

If something is lost, it is the birth of a new gain.

When the heart is unclouded by needs and
surrendered in the trust that life is benevolent,
the surge of the river of life moving through us
will always guide us to the highest choice.

Power and innocence are two sides of one coin.
Innocence can only be found by living in the moment
and it is in the moment where power is found.

Humans' greatest fear is their own inner silence –
the place where all unresolved trauma reveals itself.
Facing oneself in silence is a threshold that must be
crossed for the peace of mastery to be birthed.

The growth sought by many is illusory. The unreal form cannot be growing, and the formless One Life does not need to.

A surrendered life, free from strife, receives the abundance that Source provides.

Whether we struggle toward awakening or permit it to come effortlessly, every understanding comes at the exact moment intended by the One Life.

It is through asking for what we want, while appreciating what we have, that we live the most powerful law of abundance.

There is only the now – the place where all truth is accessible. Through the interconnectedness of life, what is known by one is available to all.

Living our highest truth always benefits all.

Creation is a dream, for in the One Life individuation can never be. In full cooperation with the Infinite, it becomes a pleasant dream.

The heart does not open until the mind has been silenced. Only then will the infinite preciousness of life reveal itself.

Noise pulls us from this moment into the next, where linear time resides. Treasure moments of silence: they allow the tension of linear time to leave your body.

Letting go of predictability allows us to become
the contradiction: formlessness and form.

Humility is not to believe you are less than another. That
merely pays homage to the other's arrogance. Humility
is acknowledging the every life has equal value.

Create a sacred space by expressing passionately.
The denser you find your environment, the greater the
need to push the density back with your passion.

Through knowing timelessness, life slows
that we may experience its depth.

When you stop thinking about your past
and defining yourself from your past – then
boundlessness and abundance will come.

To study the concept of adventure within the deep peace
of Oneness, we hide what we know. Designing moments
that trigger knowingness, we discover it yet again.

In pretended freedom of choice, we forget
that the dreamer designs the dream.

The past cannot hold more value than the present.
Why then do we look back? The present is a worthy
edifice built from the bricks of past moments.

Rich in the timeless embrace of self-nurturing, the Earth
cradles and comforts one who approaches in reverence.

The idle fill the air with chatter. The master embraces in silence the contradiction of his being.

Body programs are not real. It is the One Life that is keeping the body in place. It does not have to eat, sleep or breathe to exist.

Habits are unreal since no past, or memory, or patterns exist; thus they are robbed of the elements from which they could be formed.

The student asks, "What can I take?", while
the master asks, "How can I best serve?"

There's no such thing as non-life enhancing since
everything serves a purpose, otherwise it wouldn't exist.

In transient emphasis, every life form shines.

Let our lives be like a feather on the wind:
unattached to outcome, knowing no point of
arrival, and free from self-reflection.

Nothing has ever been out of control in life. It
just seems so from our small vantage point.

When life and death are overcome, life's changes are
effortlessly accomplished. The need for the drastic
changes of death, that shocks the soul, become obsolete.

In every life form, all of existence plays
out the intent of the One Life.

Suffering is only inherent in life when we engage
in its movement. In the stillness of full surrender,
we enter into the peace of timelessness.

There is no form of work more important than another
when all is done as an offer of love upon the altar of life.

A mistake is an insight you have
just hidden from yourself.

Abundant resources become ours when we leave the
movement of life, which is time. Through surrender,
we become the still point and all comes to us.

The mind creates mirrors, then fights against them.
When we wait in stillness, all life reveals itself to us.

Peace in the world comes from peace within.
Peace within comes from the inner marriage of our masculine and feminine into perfect oneness.

Life beyond the senses becomes
incorruptible in its purity.

Density does not exist. One area of the ocean cannot be more dense than another within the indivisibility of life.

Truth is all that exists and it is the foundation of life. Illusion is the temporary tool of truth.

Nothing can cause over-focus or hypnotism, for there is no reference point within the vastness to focus upon and no mind to focus.

The mountains of timelessness dream of the ages. With tiptoed steps, the moments walk toward timelessness.

A miracle is where cause and effect are one.

The key to stepping off the moving wheel of
linear time into the stillness of the One Life, is
to release the concept of relationship through the
understanding that there is only One Being.

Think of money as love. Give feely where
you can and it will return freely.

As we awaken to our true heritage to find we are all that is, we come directly in touch with the magic of all life.

There is no need to justify the existence
of our form; it is there for our delight – an
embryo waiting to become great things.

Living as the One Life is the greatest
contribution we can make to the whole.

The shallow accessing of life is no better than engaging it deeply. All parts of the ocean are equally valid.

Unhurried by the folly of expectation, life stirs in its mantle of timelessness.

The ultimate goal of the evolution of the monetary system is that we offer goods or services for what they are intrinsically worth to us in trade – a voluntary trade system.

Moments, like tears of joy of the Infinite,
are bestowed as priceless gifts. Like pearls,
they lie on the chest of timelessness.

Living within the Infinite's Being is to live in
the fullness of an inexhaustible supply.
Acknowledging the never-ending Source of
abundance increases its accessibility.

Bliss is the laughter of the Infinite in our cells.

Life is completely safe because nothing hostile can exist within the Infinite. Life in a rut demands forced change because it has to match the spontaneity of Eternal Life.

There can be no continuity in an ever-unfolding existence. Every moment is new when seen from the One Life.

If we hear the Holy Song of all we encounter, everything we touch turns to gold.

There is no ability for anything to get stuck or for repetition to occur. Life has only spontaneous innovation.

The master asks, "How can I best serve?", whereas the god asks, "What joy awaits?"

In knowing the cells and organs to be unnecessary parts of the eternal, fluid field of the body, youthening is restored.

The communities of the future will function from a trust system in which all put their products and services to use and only take what they need.

Inner conflict dissolves in the knowing that there is nothing to achieve, only enjoyment.

We think we discover the new, but what we have discovered is the eternal newness with which life expresses every moment.

There are no questions – only unfolding revelations.

Recognizing form to be a specific emphasis of beingness allows us to masterfully de-emphasize discordance and emphasize harmony.

If we see ourselves as a field, there is no healing necessary.

Through surrender we are at one with
the currents of life. Only then can we
surf the waves of opportunity.

As life changes from a lower order to a higher
one, power is released. Change is therefore the
bringer of great gifts and should be welcomed.

In exquisite sensitivity of awareness, life
responds by unveiling its real beauty.

Nothing can be a mistake with the Infinite,
not even density. It provides an embryonic
sac for the creation of delight.

The existing unfoldment of life is not noticeable
because all life moves and changes at once. This
creates no reference point by which to measure
change. Life is completely new each moment.

All you see that is praiseworthy can become an active
part of you. If it were not already slumbering within,
you would not be able to recognize it without.

We think we carry the weight of the ages, but
to the One Life, only a moment has passed.

Supreme experiences and divine revelations await
the one who rests in the deep peace of surrender.

A moment suspended in time is called home
to the endless ocean of timelessness.

True beauty, though seldom uncovered, changes the discoverer forever as it peeks through the veils of illusion.

Yeats said: "Where beauty has no ebb, decay no flood, but joy is wisdom, time an endless song…" Only in timelessness can this be so. Only there is the Song of the Infinite expressing and not drowned out by the discordance of time.

In an existence of perfection, there is nothing to change; there is nothing power is needed for. We are supported by the One Life.

The slow awakening of life is part of the
Infinite's symphony of delight.

Damage cannot touch us as part of the
Incorruptible One Life. There is no way
to fracture or divide the ocean.

One area of the ocean can be no denser than
another. Bodies are merely an image of fluid
fields within our true vastness of the One Life.

There is no truth to seek, just answers to realize. All things reveal themselves to those who are ready.

Many dream of a point of arrival for their journey, neglecting to see that the only point of arrival is the present moment.

The past is a dream in a reality where time does not exist. The future is no more than an unexplored wish. The present is a well-earned gift.

Life supplies the one who knows
his limitless bounty.

We dwell in incorruptible holy matter. It is the
substance of all life. All we have to do is remember it.

Speak not to manipulate, control or persuade, but
let your words be free from attached outcome.

Bodies are made to play the game of movement. The Infinite dances through bodies to the symphony of its Being.

The Infinite never needed to prod life to grow through pain and It never has.

Slumbering in the womb of creation, each was given a personal matrix that acted as our individual incubation chamber.

We get our wishes only half the time. State your wishes, but rejoice in what life brings or happiness can only be there half the time.

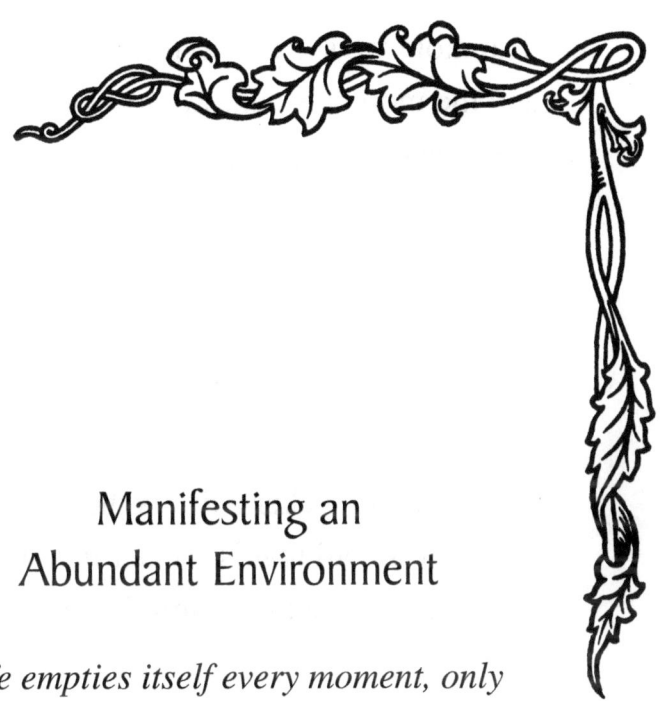

Manifesting an Abundant Environment

Life empties itself every moment, only to be filled again. When we fluidly match this ever-new regeneration we can, through grateful enjoyment, call forth what makes our hearts sing.

The more we see the divinity within others and the more we acknowledge oneness, the more another's unique gifts become ours.

In each light-seeker's life is the knowledge that they are all that is. To act in a way that is life-enhancing to self, benefits all.

From loyalty, blindness is born. See others in your environment anew each day that you not keep them captive by indulging their folly.

Do not forget the width and the height of your vision
when you are amongst those that are without it.

There are only two choices in the cosmos: what is
more life-enhancing and what is most life-enhancing.

Send a blessing with the money you spend, that it
may bless the fisherman and statesman alike.

Thought pulls us out of the moment into the past or future. It disturbs innocence, since innocence is only found in the moment.

A life well-lived is like climbing a mountain; every new moment is the highest point of your life.

Some, unaware that they create their own life experiences, say 'if only'. Others, having refined themselves through experiential wisdom, say, 'next time'.

Let your speech be a cause rather than the
effect of another's speech. It is masterful
to respond and foolish to react.

Excellence cannot be an occasional visitor. It has
to be a constant companion. It will then invite
additional guests: opportunity, success and increase.

There are those who speak in circles and those
who speak in a straight line. Listen to the
meaning behind the circle and feel the meaning
behind the obvious of the straight line.

Do this day the tasks allotted for it, but live as though you have eternity. Mortality and linear time are only illusions.

Be lavish with yourself with those things that bring you joy.

Only the blind believe they have multiple choices in life. The wise know there is only one viable choice in every situation: that which is most life-enhancing.

To not trust the infallibility of your environment
is to question your ability to infallibly sustain
yourself. Your environment is just a mirror.

Because we are in oneness with our environment,
over-balanced desire-based emotions cause areas of
global-flooding. Under-balanced emotions of grateful
recognition cause the eroding of global snow-packs.
We balance the planet by balancing ourselves.

The Dream has refined the cosmos in its incubation
stages. The tools of the Dream were space and
time. These can now be released with gratitude.

Find the true pleasures of life. Man, having lost touch with what brings him joy, substitutes the veneer of purchased sophistication.

In times of scarcity, know it to be a temporary regrouping that will reveal what really matters.

Life's fertility wanes when there's egocentricity. Spontaneous giving of the self creates an environment in which to flourish.

The evolution into a voluntary barter and trade system must begin with us – even if it is just one step at a time.

Education is the navigation of the mind-made maze of man that acquaints us with its stale information. Stimulated learning is the remembering of the all-knowingness of the self – the seat of effortless genius.

Money is crystallized power and the same laws apply. When it is hoarded, the universe conspires to take it away.

Change as unfoldment can come in a moment. In knowing this, we can see it, and in seeing it, others will too.

The monetary system uses counterfeit value, pretending paper money has value. It must evolve to a barter system and beyond.

Attempting to right a wrong judges and divides. Acknowledging wholeness uplifts through the interconnectedness of all life.

Linear growth is obsolete. Exponential growth comes in an instant through the flowering of the heart. Growth no longer comes through overcomings, but by embracing wholeness.

Send blessings with your work that the fruits of your labor may have increased value and leave the cosmos in your debt.

Trust in the resilience and ingenuity of man, and in one lending a helping hand to another to successfully navigate a global recession.

A life of mastery is comprised of belief and faith.
Believe in the infallibility of your actions as long
as you live your highest truth. Faith knows that
good intentions will ultimately benefit all.

For the masses, the primary quest of life is self-
avoidance; yet, through our environment we stand
revealed. In the infallible appearance of the dawn, we
find the hope that springs eternally from our hearts.

We have no real personal choice, other than the
quality of the moment – how well we live it, how
much we see it and how much we enjoy it.

Give lavishly whenever you can. The right question to ask is "What is the most I can give?" rather than "What is the most I can get for the least I can give?"

One of the greatest resources of guidance is found in the signs in our environment. Failing to heed them or to become literate in their language is tragic.

Most waste energy wishing their lives would change. Masters change their environment by changing themselves.

Time management is essential when demands
increase. Use a structured and disciplined
approach, leaving time for fun with loved ones.

By doing your work with a glad heart, as a service
to life, you become a cause rather than an effect.

In taking time for deep meaningful living,
like watching the dawn, we know our joy. Joy
is the guidance system for our choices.

Achievement driven action is polarity-based and therefore comes at a cost. There is no cost for accentuating qualities in our environment by expressing them. If we wish to have abundance, let us be the epitome of abundance.

Do not let work dictate the pace of your life. Dedicate time slots in which you respond to its demands. In this way it does not become the master and you the slave.

The essence of abundant living is found in generosity of expression, not in depleting our environment by taking more than we need.

See life as a spontaneous dance of joy, not
a fixed maze through which you have to
find your way with perseverance.

Create in whatever measure you can, a
work and living environment that expresses
reverence for the sacredness of life.

Linear time and linear becoming have in reality
never existed. We are free to powerfully affect
the fluid unfolding of the moment through the
purity of our intent, without the bondage of
time's delay between cause and effect.

To live an impeccable life promotes that
which is life-enhancing for all.

When we labor with joy and excellence, drudgery to
earn a living turns to a labor of love and creativity.

Directional power through impressing others
with its miracles is limited – the tool of
those who wish to persuade. Inclusive power
that changes the world by changing the self
benefits all life and is therefore limitless.

The one who knows himself to be all, creates for others in his presence, the holy sanctuary of full acceptance.

What we focus on, we solidify. What we experience without expectations, unfolds into endless possibilities.

To oppose life is to fight images on a screen. You are the projector and your attitudes form the film. Change those and your environment will change too.

Causes within the Dream do not create an effect.
The One Life does. When we cease trying
to affect life, miracles flow through us.

We believe we can change independently
from our environment. But we are all
things. When we change, all changes.

What is real is incorruptible and changeless.
Through the falseness of form, the real
shines through and the One Life glows.

Your possessions are your stewardship.
Repair them rather than discarding, that the
garbage heaps on Earth may dwindle.

Re-invent life daily, that fresh authenticity might
be the quality of your journey. Pause during your
activities that the quiet recognition of divine
perfection might reveal itself and lead you on.

Interacting with our fellow man provides inspiration
if we look for it. Communion with nature
awakens the silent foundation of our being.

Wherever there is division, there is illusion.
Whenever something can be defined, it is unreal.

The more you provide heaven on Earth at home, the more stark the contrast when the child goes to school. Yet the solace of a loving, cherishing environment to come home to, is a source of great strength in the face of the often brutal atmosphere of school.

Life around us lies in intermingled fields of possibilities that come alive only when the song of our lives stimulates them into existence.

We often feel responsible for maintaining harmony
in our environment. From the large picture, there
is only harmony, thus nothing to maintain.

When resources are scarce, let innovation blossom. This
in itself, can be a form of creativity shared with others.

Scientists have found we entrain the Earth and
vice versa. When we cultivate fertile gardens,
the Earth restores our fertile abundance.

Layers of illusion will not release until their value
is seen. Acceptance is the beginning of change.

The unreal cannot affect the real, which is incorruptible.
Nothing in the environment needs be protected against.

We hesitate to act before we can ensure a beneficial
outcome. All outcomes are beneficial, for we
dwell in the benevolence of the Infinite.

There is no such thing as reciprocity. The benefit is in the giving, for all giving is to self.

Like a child, intimidated by his own endless progression of images in dual mirrors, we feel diminished by the vastness of ourselves reflected in our environment. But as the originating source of our reality, when we change, all changes.

No history exists. No future awaits. Just the moment that stretches into eternity.

Change as unfoldment can come in a moment. In knowing this, we can bring it about. Through the miracles of our lives, we set others free as well.

When we change our perception,
our environment changes.

The world around you is not your creation, but your expression. As you express passionately and abundantly that which makes your heart sing, your environment must deliver its abundance likewise.

Look for truth everywhere. Even a clock that does not work is right twice a day. The biggest fool may yet reveal the highest wisdom.

Doing the same activities every day constricts energy, so be wary of habits and strive to break them.

In at-oneness with the One Life we cancel out illusion in our environment, always dwelling in sacred space.

In an ocean of divine compassion, I endlessly frolic,
renewed in each moment by Divine Intent.

If we can live one moment gloriously and
then, the next and the next - greatness is
born. But it comes one choice at a time.

Living from the heart produces the unpredictable
spontaneity mind would deny us.

A master with authenticity embraces life.

Apathy is the key ingredient of mediocrity.
Greatness watches for moments in which
a contribution to life can be made.

Treat money with respect. It is the thread that
weaves together the tapestry of human societies.

Prayer has been used through eons to fulfill our agendas. It is a redundant concept when we are eternally guided by the Infinite's song of perfection.

When we do everything from a sense of great adventure, we are aligned with the very purpose of created life.

Humility is recognizing that within the mystery of the Infinite's being, all are equal.

Every being contributes a unique equation that enhances understanding of the mystery of beingness. If one number is removed from the equation then it no longer works.

The adventure of life is like riding an ocean wave or shooting the rapids. It is meant to be exhilarating and inspiring; a journey of unpredictable delights.

Let us live life as a spontaneous expression, not as a set of guidelines we need to know. Then at last, our futile search for truth will cease.

Reverent appreciation honors the perfection of all life. It acknowledges the beauty of the moment, knowing that each is unique and a special creative expression of All That Is.

When action has no agenda, doingness and beingness become one. Restful repose slumbers in work and work becomes work no more.

In ceasing to strive, the moment embraces you. In seeing the perfection behind appearances, you enter through the gates of timelessness and all becomes possible.

The need for external laws to govern inner man
implies that he is an effect of circumstances
rather than the expression of the One Life.

Community can be a blessing or a chain that binds. It is
only a tool meant to serve the individuals within it, not a
tyrant demanding that they wear the mask of conformity.

Environment can serve as a reflection of what
we are because it is us. It is just a peculiarity
of our vision that we see it as separate.

When we heal our bodies, we heal the Earth.

The Earth groans under the weight of refuse from prepared food containers. Returning to whole foods is not only economical, but a return to conscious living.

A production line can become a mantra when our attitude is one of voluntary service to all life.

When we attempt to right a wrong, it divides because we have placed a judgment on it as not being in alignment with the divine will of the One Life. However, if we acknowledge the wholeness of a circumstance or person, it will uplift and heal.

Language by nature, is separation-based. Anything that can be described is therefore an illusion. Experience, in silence, the Oneness.

Deny not error in your brother, but rather see it as a guiding mechanism to steer you in another direction.

There is neither past nor future and progression is no longer cyclical. Awareness no longer moves in spirals, but responds to love, praise and gratitude.

All are innocently performing their
part on the stage of life.

The bondage of the dream that we have blood-families to which we owe obligations must be closely examined. Our true family is where our joy and inspiration lies.

Everything has a part to play in the orchestration of the dance, guiding our feet in this direction or that.

Expressing one's need should become unified with consideration for others.

Many suppress their gifts because of the mistaken assumption that they carry with them the responsibility of saving or serving mankind.

Personality is but a coping mechanism within the illusionary spider webs of creation.

Engage wholeheartedly in the play of life but also be the observing audience, lest you forget you are not the role you are enacting.

Through self-discipline and awareness, we can perform our plays masterfully, gaining satisfaction from the roles we play.

The only place we can experience life
directly is in timelessness.

Let life be a living affirmation. Give liberally
of your praise, love and gratitude. Embrace
readily the new unfolding of life's adventure.

We heal the environment by healing ourselves. We
promote abundance by being abundant with ourselves.
If we feel guilt over having when others do not,
we deprive not only ourselves but them as well.

Knowing life to be a dream, we can become
lucid dreamers – masters of the dream
environment. Reality becomes fluid rather
than static and a life of miracles ensues.

It is in alignment with the moment that the Infinite
Intent can flow through us. Aligned with Infinite Intent,
we live in the most life-enhancing way possible.

We reach for beauty, which fosters greed. We
acknowledge our true beauty and it becomes multiplied.

Appreciation is the overwhelming thankfulness that streams from us when we are touched by an individual act or experience. The unexpected call from a busy husband who just wants to hear your voice, the exuberant hug from a child rushing home from school, can trigger this glow of recognition and appreciation.

The Abundant Self

The dancing feet have no volition of their own, but are directed by the dancer. Living from the greater self restores abundant grace to the life of the little self.

Life changes yet does not change. In its unfolding, one form yields to another. Though it may seem destructive, there is only spontaneous perfection.

We are like doorways for Infinite compassion. To love others before self-love is not possible because it is self-love that opens the door of the heart.

Become sensitive to your promptings from within. Disregarding them and then blaming external sources for your depletion, is not masterful.
Play when it is time, work when it is required, for you write the script of your own life.

The body in its true state is not subject to death. Only when its light is not coupled with luminosity can it die. Luminosity expresses through authentic living.

Supported by all life, overwhelming odds cannot exist. A master accesses all perspectives at once.

The dance of life is a consuming sensual interaction with self. The union with another is but a further expression of the same.

We dishonor the journey of our lives by not acknowledging the worth of our seeming errors as our greatest teachers of wisdom.

There is only Self – all else is a mirror.

What can be loved but Self? What can be embraced but life? The love of life is merely the exuberant expression of Self and thus all there is, is the One.

Many identify themselves by the experiences of the past.
Others define themselves by what they are becoming.

∞

All self-perception is a lens into the Infinite's perception.

∞

The only discovery is self-discovery, which we express,
through our experiences, as increased enjoyment.

The real part of you consists of emotions of recognition of Infinite qualities expressed in life.

Hiding the next moment from ourselves, we discover it anew.

Consciousness is not something you seek, nor is it something you await. Consciousness is already yours.

Power is an irrevocably fused component of
the incorruptible holy matter from which we
are made. It is our inseparable birthright.

No questions to answer, nor mysteries to see.
I am the Paradox. The Paradox am I.

Self-expression cannot be when the self does not
exist, if there is only one Being in Existence.

The one who speaks, cannot listen. Life whispers its mysteries into the ear of one who listens in silence.

Roles can be assumed to aid in manifesting intent. They only obscure truth when we believe them to be all that we are.

The duty of one is to preserve the sanctity of the heart and the stillness of the mind. In this way, one can then render the highest service.

No man is truly free who wears the mask of identity.

The light-seeker is always ready to embrace the truth of the moment and to change directions in order to follow the adventure of self-discovery.

We cannot rewrite the madness of the world by being immersed in it. Create of your life a sanctuary, for only from reverent silence can you change the world.

Solitude is the beginning of greatness. It is the place where we meet the Infinite One.

It isn't what you do that counts, it is who you are. By being who you are and vibrating at that frequency, you can affect all of creation.

Laughing at oneself keeps one from succumbing to the pompous preening of self-importance.

The needs of appetites are disciplined by seeing
them for what they are: substitutes for areas
in which we have abandoned ourselves.

Relinquishing the little self, I become the One Life.

If for just this moment, we can see ourselves as being
the center of the cosmos; as having the ability to
influence with the quality of our thoughts the very
fabric of existence, what would we contribute?

That which we seek to understand about ourselves
is not that which is waiting to be learnt, but
that which is waiting to be expressed.

Choose as companions those who make you feel
augmented and who inspire you to excel. As you
grow, shed with grace those who do not.

Masters have nothing to prove and everything to discover.

In the quest for the discovery of self, some seek it in others. The sage seeks it in the metaphysics of the cosmos. Both are equally valid in revealing the never-ending mystery of life.

Daydreams, as well as fantasy, arise to fill the gaps of our life where we have abandoned ourselves. They are surrogates for life.

Incorruptible and timeless, we have forever to enjoy the never-ending adventure of self-discovery.

The student seeks truth. The master creates
truth spontaneously in the moment.

Live your life as a cause, not an effect. Respond only
when and if necessary. Fools react, masters respond.

You cannot fly high like an eagle while simultaneously
trying to fit in with the turkeys. Moving beyond
mortal boundaries requires an uncompromising life.

There is no need for self-work or for the elimination of illusions from ourselves. Illusions are merely a timing mechanism to guide us through the dance.

My self-imposed boundaries dissolve.

Do not defend yourself. What need is there for one who dwells in the innocence of the One Life to prove that it is so? Nothing but innocence exists.

Within the all-present life, and from the vastness
of our being, we can discover the self by studying
it in the ever-changing gems of our bodies.

There is only one choice in the cosmos: what is
life-enhancing. Choose from your largest identity
rather than from your lowest limitations or fears.

All are engaged in a grand adventure of epic proportions;
the discovery of self on the edge of newness.

Let deep self-reverence fill our being as we accept the holy origins of ourselves as part of the One Life of incorruptibility.

I am delighted by my unfolding existence.

Self-knowledge precedes self-love. But the only self-knowledge we can ever have is that we are an infallible and pure instrument of the One Life.

The One in forgetfulness is trapped in a world
of opposite appearances. The master knows the
illusions and dances with the contradictions of life
to avoid having his or her awareness trapped.

We feel self-important when we know something
someone else does not. But all answers come from
Infinite Life; we receive it exactly when we need it.

Imagination is inspired by acknowledgement
of the gifts of the moment.

Because the cosmos is a benign place, there
is only one place where courage applies
- living from ruthless self-honesty.

You are the center of your cosmos. With all the power
of your vast existence, let every touch and every
word convey compassion and blessings. In this way,
you place the crown of sovereignty on your head.

Speak only when your heart prompts you to do so.
Only then will your words be androgynous in nature.
In this way, you speak the language of Infinite Life.

I am changeless change and I live from an
eternal perspective in the moment.

The Infinite vastness and grandeur only feels
overwhelming when we see ourselves as separate from it.
The truth is that what we are experiencing is ourselves.

Regrets come only when growth has occurred. Many
would forfeit their past foolish actions, but then
the growth those actions brought would have to be
given up as well. Embrace your seeming folly as
your greatest gift – it was a teacher in disguise.

What is reality but aspects of the Self revealed?
It can be changed by acknowledging greater
parts of the self, previously unseen.

To forgive others assumes guilt. True forgiveness knows
there is nothing to forgive. No one can do anything
to us without our having called it in or agreed to it.

Autonomy comes not from wanting freedom of
choice – we have only One Life and we are part of
its expression. Autonomy is living in the Oneness.

I am the catalyst for rapturous and miraculous living.

Trust comes from knowing we are connected to Source. Courage comes from extending beyond the boundaries of our comfort zone to the place where all new knowledge is gained.

The illusion of being incomplete creates the illusion of achievement. There is no achievement when there is no choice.

I dwell in the eternal peace of integrated cooperation.

Like dancing shadows on the wall, is life
to the one who sees with eyes alone.

The One Life speaks with one voice. The
only reason anything can speak to us is
because it is us speaking to ourselves.

I live in indivisible oneness.

A life that flourishes is one that allows the new to effortlessly unfold through it, while maintaining an eternal perspective.

In your heart is the living temple of the Infinite where today's truth cannot be tomorrow's truth.

The hollows carved in your soul by the winters of your life are the fertile hollows where seeds of joy can grow. The master never envies the one who lives a seasonless life where seeds have to grow in shallow ground.

Inner stillness is necessary so that when our answer arrives, we are able to hear it.

May we overcome the egoic self; an identity based on the body, emotions and mind. May it dissolve itself so that we may remember that we are the One expressing as the many.

Many shun desires as ungodly, but desires are the seeds of the future. It is only when they are wholly self-oriented that they become unholy needs.

Life spins on a single point. Each of us is such a pivot point, impacting the whole with every action in every moment.

The warrior's purpose is to vigilantly guard the authenticity of his life, guarding against all external and internal programming.

Feeling unlovable, many settle for feeling
needed. Lovingly parent your inner child,
for it is the birthplace of self-worth.

Self-confidence assumes incorrectly that it
must create what it needs. Humility recognizes
the self as a conduit for eternal flow.

A master welcomes pain as well as joy, and sees in pain
but another opportunity to triumph over resistance to life.

What we attempt to control will produce
volatility instead. The only control we
may ever have is self-control.

There are those who build and those who tear down.
What makes the difference is not being afraid to fail.

I am here simply to express, not to consider
others' opinions. To do so is to pander
to the unreality of the dream.

We empower what we focus on. Define
yourself through every action as the master
you are and you shall surely embody it.

Total self-responsibility and absolute freedom are two
sides of one coin. One cannot exist without the other.

Work is nothing more than the delightful
opportunity to make the day better for self
and for the self hiding in others.

The most immediate way to gain power is to see what you have never seen before. Seeing further than your surface mind can grasp will set you free from its tyranny.

Illusion as entertainment demands the price of pain. Self-acknowledged perfection is an eternal surprise.

Some shun riches because they can entrap the awareness of man; others wear poverty like a badge of righteousness. But they are one – for as long as we live a life of opposites through judgment, what gains we have bring with them certain losses.

When tension is an age-old companion, man becomes addicted to it and seeks relationships that produce tension and creates emergencies to react to. Take time just to be.

Truth is what a master spontaneously brings to each moment, whereas a student spends his life searching for that which is outside of himself.

Death has no place in the fabric of existence – the incorruptible holy matter of the Infinite's Being. The master savors the one fluid moment that never ends.

Seeking yourself in the similarities of others
binds you both to the mediocrity of sameness.
Uniformity stifles growth and is the death knell of
greatness. It binds not only yourself, but another
by the bands of your selective affirmation.

Comfort zones are the boundaries of
your defense mechanisms.

To live life half-heartedly, to give – but not too
much, to open one's heart only when it is safe,
is to live in the half-light of existence.

The quest of man is to search for truth.
To become filled with wisdom, insight and
light is naught but a search for self.

The changing of the cosmos from a caterpillar into a
butterfly may seem catastrophic, but only from Infinite
vision can the perfection of the changes be seen.

One's first duty is to preserve the sanctity of the
heart and the stillness of the mind. In this way,
one can then render the highest service.

If you have become a stranger to passion, find its
tracks within your joy. The deeper you go into joy,
the more your passion will reveal itself, for they
are partners in the joyous discovery of life.

The consciousness of an individual is determined by
how much of life's resources his attitudes permit him to
access. All life consists of an infinite supply of resources.

For those who resist life, time moves linearly
like an arrow. For those who do not gain the
insights of experiences, they repeat themselves
in cyclical fashion like a wheel.

Addiction occurs when the self is abandoned.

You are the underpinning of life when you live from excellence, from a grand and glorious vision and the majesty of your being.

We are heirs to the Kingdom of the One Life, not beggars at the gate. We often put up with the dysfunctional and unacceptable as though we do not deserve better, thereby dishonoring the divinity that expresses through us as our life.

In the adventure of life, we are required to perform many roles. In believing them to be real, they become identities. Identity traps awareness and hinders spiritual evolution.

A master cannot afford to indulge even the smallest blind spot in his or her vision. A grain of sand is not small in the mechanism of a watch.

If you would find your strong suits, seek them in your weaknesses. It is in overcoming them that your greatest strengths will be forged.

Criticism is born of self-hatred. The pain
you feel is the approval you withhold.

Do not feed attention to the beauty standards of the
world as they are designed to make us feel inferior.
The true standard of beauty is the purity of our intent.

Unfoldment seems as movement, but that
is just an illusory trick of the senses. There
is no movement because there is no space
or direction in the Being of the One.

The flow of life is not movement. That is an illusion due to successively accentuating ever-existing fields like the notes played on a piano.

One cannot escape the matrix of illusion by affirming oneself by the standards of the matrix. A master is self-affirming for approval.

There can be no hierarchy of knowledge when it is defined as the effortless knowing of the moment – a gift available to all.

Because we are a being as vast as the cosmos,
to fear another is to fear our self.

The greatest freedom to strive for is freedom from
thinking that anything can be bound by the unreal.

We design the games of life by hiding parts
of perception; if you don't like the game,
reclaim the perception and play another.

Wisdom is the addiction of the master who,
having stepped beyond the existing paradigm,
uses it as a frame of reference. Afraid of his own
vastness, he reaches for yesterday's truth.

There can be no such thing as order when it is defined as structure. It is only a tool of control created by the mind.

Incredible diversity awaits one who lives
the depth of all dream cycles.

One who lives authentically from the heart is self-referring for approval. To such a one, leadership as a means of persuading others is meaningless. He or she simply shines like the brightest star in the sky and others, seeing such a light, are inspired to find their own.

Complete self-fulfillment comes from contented repose within labor.

There can be no such thing as chaos. No flaws in the One Being exist. Chaos is but the way we describe that which defies our understanding.

Fallacies and belief systems must be eliminated;
we assist others and ourselves by living
our highest truth in each moment.

Predictability is an obstacle to greatness
that binds us to past standards.

Self-centeredness occurs when the outer senses
dominate. Outer and inner senses must merge and
experience life from the largest perspective: a being
as vast as the cosmos having a human experience.

The vast number of inner senses, consisting
of pure emotions and states of being, provide
a far greater wealth of guidance as to what is
life-enhancing than the five outer senses.

To pacify reason and its need for complexity
is to disrespect the effortless instinctual
knowing of the greater self.

Life as a reflection is an obsolete concept. All forms of
life, even inanimate objects, are made from the Infinite's
Being and therefore alive and real. All lives within us.

Accessing the deeper layers of beingness, by seeing through the gates of the cycles, is to live beyond the shallowness of face value.

The cycles of the Dream are windows into the depths of the self.

Planning creates a container or mold for life to fill. Plans can become traps when we rigidly hold onto them.

Leadership consists of self-responsibility. All life can be changed through proxy by one who knows this to be so. The goal of life is that all become leaders.

Self-responsibility brings freedom, for with it comes more self-determination.

You may feel like a tiny speck in the vastness of the cosmos. Never forget that you are the cosmos.

Deterioration is only present when there is opposition to life. The true nature of life is incorruptible.

To live from the greater self is to overcome the tyranny of disease. The ailment can be gone in a minute if we see ourselves as the One Life.

The initiate knows he can change his environment by changing himself. The master knows no difference, but enjoys his environment as himself.

Self-confidence comes from the ego-identification of the smaller self. Self-trust comes from knowing our infallibility as the One Life.

Greater than discoveries of the wonders of the world, is the adventure of self-discovery.

All programmed behavior must dissolve by allowing the fluid expression of the Infinite through us. This includes the conditioned expectations of how to express maleness or femaleness.

No one is truly free who wears the mask of
identity. He becomes a puppet in the hands of
others, who feed his ego-identification.

The all-knowledge and skill of the One Life
is ours to draw upon. That learning is needed
to accomplish excellence is an illusion.

Hidden treasures of omni-sensory perception
await and flower with our attention.

Personal desire is an emotional attachment to outcome.
Once we are free of personal desires we can become
a clear instrument of the divine will of spirit.

The shadows in our lives are cast by unyielded
potential – the result of living a life of opposites. To
live in oneness is to live a shadowless existence.

When instinctual knowing is not present, too
much speed can create shallow living and too
much depth can produce stagnation.

If you give what does not feel good
to you, you become a martyr.

When we live a programmed life, like a moth in a spider web, we cannot tell when another strand of subliminal programming captures us. Freedom from conditioning will reveal the intrusion of another's thoughts.

We live in the timelessness of the One Life,
freed from the bondage of mind and space.

There can be no abandonment. The real eternal part of us is at all times participating in full knowingness throughout our lives.

Form and time are connected like two wings of the imaginary bird of linear progression. When we live in no-time, we become unattached to form.

From the endless ocean of Beingness, the vastness brought this beauty to form my body. Everywhere I go I take my body with me.

Fear of relinquishing the body is fear of freedom, like a captive afraid of the unknown outside his cell.

The body lures us into thinking we know. It gives the illusion of a reference point within eternal flow.

In total surrender do we find timelessness.
In timelessness, do we find ourselves.

There is no need for overcoming past illusions from our lives. Illusions are merely a timing mechanism to guide us through the dance. When it is time for them to dissolve, it will be obvious.

My body becomes a new creation as the gifts of the moment reveal themselves through me.

Even if the illusory form should die, as long as we know without a doubt that we are not that which is corruptible, another shall immediately form in its place.

The Abundant Self

When something is seen as 'harmful', it means you have separated yourself from that which it represents. This makes it an opposite and opposites bring opposition.

The joy of our being must contain within itself its own passion, that our roots and wings may be lived as one.

It is within the innocent discovery of life that the master is born. Let our mantra be, 'I know nothing. I experience all things in the timelessness of my being'.

The illumination that life is an experience,
not a set of guidelines to live by, dissolves
the prison erected by the need to know.

Because reality is a mirror, he who
controls himself, controls his world.

No self-approval is needed for we have been
created for the sake of joy. There is nothing to
accomplish other than deep enjoyment of life.

The one whose identity is based on what he does,
is like a traveler in an unknown land, navigating
the way forward by a map of where he has been.

Any perceived shadow we fight against is cast
by its own light. Our transparent luminosity is
unable to let light through when it is cluttered
by the occlusions of belief systems.

Our bodies cannot be incarcerated when our spirits
are free. We can only be imprisoned by beliefs.

Eliminate the illusion of pace that the
sweetness of life may be discovered.

When we think of the past as real rather than a dream,
we become trapped by cords of association.

The difference between a conscious person and
one who is not, is that in one the resources of life
are expressed, while in the other they are latent.

The timing of the dance of life is orchestrated by what seem to be delays. But flawless is the timing of the steps of the dance. Knowing this, how can we be anything other than patient?

We have but slept and dreamt that we were separate. We have never been separate.

Personal history is the story we tell ourselves. Personal identity is the role we play within that story.

Any person revealing issues to you is mirroring
something within yourself. This is why
you have come to learn, not to teach.

Begin attracting abundance by giving to yourself
those things that money cannot buy.

Greatness requires solitude. Mediocrity is
fed by the communion of the masses. To be
outstanding one cannot run with the pack.

Masters do not rely on belief, but rather on effortless knowing. The greatest stumbling blocks to learning are belief systems and worldviews.

Power is seldom seen by the one who wields it, for it is not the few cheap tricks others marvel at called miracles. Instead, it is the pivoting of reality from our self as the center of our universe; a change too vast to see from our vantage point.

Filling our hearts with reverence and awe at the beauty of life helps us to discover our own flawlessness.

If neither the fear of the future nor the
pain of the past any longer rules our lives,
we have become sovereign beings.

The nature of individuated life is conflict
and opposition. Only in knowing ourselves
to be the One Being can we find peace.

I flourish through connecting with the
inspiration of my unfathomable depths.

To find worth in others is to find it in our selves. To praise is to walk with reverent awareness through life.

Abundance in Expression

We dwell within the Infinite's Being where all potential is immediately available to the extent we are willing to receive it. The necessity to grow is a fallacy. Surrendered allowing is the criterion of fulfilled mastery.

The mists of life do not conceal life from
us, but rather through their contrast with the
rays of light, are what reveals it to us.

The ocean of consciousness that each one is does not
bemoan its losses or rejoice in its gains. The ocean in its
fullness, ebbs and flows in an endless expression of itself.

We are a tapestry of many colors, yet it is
woven from one multicolored thread of
the One expressing as the many.

Reverence for life is its own reward. Appreciative awareness opens the treasure chest of existence to reveal its wondrous array of gems in the form of moments.

It is in bringing joy to one's own life that we give the greatest service to humankind, because all are one. True romance is the passionate commitment to the One Life.

Linear growth is of the mind. Exponential growth comes in an instant through the flowering of the heart. Growth is not gained through overcomings, but by embracing wholeness.

The body and soul together make immortality,
but beyond them lies incorruptibility.

All life is unknowable. There is nothing
to understand, nothing to strive to become
when we are an expression of the One.

From the simplicity of the One Life as one voice,
we express through the complexity of form.

Help where you can, but do not feel guilt
about having while others do not. Uniformity
stifles a society's development.

Existing from the fullness of one's being is
an orgasmic and intimate love affair with the
profound nuances of the diverse forms of life.

Consciousness is accessible through the dynamic
balance of deep, meaningful living.

A moment well-lived changes all that has gone before.

The One Being is the ocean of possibilities.

Those who live in a way that makes their hearts sing are following the Song of Immortality. Death comes from denying the heart.

Beyond light and sound, the indescribable awaits, where form yields to the intent of a nudge from Oneness.

When our desires to express are unsupported by ourselves, they die stillborn, leaving life impoverished and our depths unexplored.

Opposition delivers perception. But if we do not take time to integrate the perception, it damages the heart. In the stillness of mind the heart finds its peace.

Books cannot prepare us for what is to come in the next spontaneous moment of unfolding life.

There is nothing that constitutes testing. We do not have to prove our right to exist when we are an expression of Infinite Life.

The beginning of wisdom is the deep conviction that because life is new every moment, we live in the unknowable.

We mistakenly honor the past as having made
us what we are in this moment. The past is but a
dream. In the moment, we are newly created.

What was excellent in the past, is mediocre in
the present. The harmonies of the beginning
of the symphony become discordant when
played in another part of the melody.

All that has gone before has brought you to
the perfection of the moment, the beginning of
timelessness and the birthplace of Eternal Life.

The attempt to dominate that which cannot be
dominated must be seen for the futility that it is.

Poetic living pushes you to be fully present in your life.

To maintain the unfoldment of the One Life,
our efforts to bring illumination to life increase
the illusion of beings of shadow. In this way the
cosmic symphony is always in harmony.

It does not matter how many hours you work if there is creativity, passion and excellence being expressed; work has changed from duty to joyous life.

Poverty has, at times, been the tool of life that encourages us to step off the treadmill of the matrix of the masses when we have not voluntarily done so.

Believe in the bounty of life and claim it as your own by living generously and avoiding hoarding.

In the place of pure spirit, growth is exponential.
To try and predict the future is to attempt
to put an exploding star in a box.

To create a new paradigm of living, simplify your life so
that the life-enhancing aspects may reveal themselves.

Poise is the crowning glory of a life well-lived
and comes in the wake of having gained an eternal
perspective amidst the many vicissitudes of life.

Authentic living in the moment transforms by proxy that which we hold dear in our heart.

As the surfer becomes the wave and the dancer becomes the drum, so the master becomes one with the currents and flow of the river of life.

By unburdening ourselves from expectations, we allow room for joyful synchronicities.

Life yields all secrets to a receptive heart
in the quietness of the mind.

There are times the tiny screw is needed, at other times
the big bolt. Each is perfect for a unique function.
There is no way to determine value other than what is
applicable moment by moment as life dances on its way.

Because there is no failure, there is no
success – just the spontaneous, exuberant
unfolding of the One Life.

Rage, fear, pain, protectiveness and guilt are but the backward images of pure emotions reflected in the mirrored walls of our chrysalis of belief systems.

Memory produces the repetition of mediocrity. Instinctual knowing guides us to excellence.

When the One expresses as the many through Its creations, it is for the purpose of being delighted.

During separation, the ability to know absolute truth was lost to the masculine. The exploration of grand adventure was lost to the feminine.

He who sits in meditation stagnates; he who strives through activity fixates on outcome.

Actions become power-laden and deliberate when they originate from the conscious realization that they affect every life form in existence.

The deep-seated fear that the One Life may behave destructively comes from seeing the destruction of the old as cataclysmic. From the large, eternal perspective, life yields gracefully to unfolding.

Nothing can ever be familiar, as life is always newly expressing.

The fear of missing something stems from the belief there is something we do not know and that it is possible to make mistakes.

In surrender, life becomes graceful.

The mundane is the setting for high adventure that has no end. In the rest provided by the ordinary, lies the springboard to catch the wind.

Because the only part of life that is real lies beyond superficial experience and our illusion of knowingness, life is forever unknowable.

Individuated life is the boundless expression of the Infinite. All limitation and lack is self-imposed and has no place in the boundlessness of our being.

The illusions of the fullness and emptiness of being eventually must dissolve – but a stepping-stone to Oneness has it been. Many ghosts of the past reside in the illusion of fullness.

Every moment we are changing life.

When change is linear, we are moved out of the innocent purity of timelessness by reaching for future potential. When change is exponential, future potential comes now.

Trauma as a way of growth is contradictory. If the aim of growth is oneness, trauma cannot deliver it, for hardship is the result of separation.

Disease and injury can come in an instant - so to can healing.

Some consider melting compassion towards all
beings to be grand, yet knowing them to be us
and all love to be self-love is even greater.

As part of the limitless Oneness, we are real and no
longer have separate movement from the whole. We move
as life moves, in a spontaneous expression of Oneness.

Reincarnation occurs because we shun parts of life.
We then vacillate throughout lifetimes between
that which we shun and that which we embrace.

In the abundant expression of authenticity shall
abundant life be restored to humanity.

It is time to go deeper into oneness, to
die to the ways of the world.

Complexity and simplicity in fact do not exist.
There is only the unfolding of Beingness that defies
description as it unfolds in the dance of the One life.

The financial dynamics of a family unit indicate its flow of power. Where the assets and monetary control is lodged, there too, is the power.

There cannot be a hierarchy of beauty when each individuated life form expresses a unique facet of unfolding life. The lily can be no more beautiful than the rose.

Loss of possessions is viewed by some as equivalent to loss of life. It is often the catalyst to deeper living and vitality.

The Infinite Oneness is androgynous;
gender is not supported by reality.

Understand death and life for the illusions
they are, but illusion does not yield to absolute
truth unless its origin is uncovered.

The fluidity of mastery is needed to stay
in step with the changes of life.

The artificial creation of the soul formed emotions; the artificial creation of the spirit formed states of being.

Reality changes without our realizing when the memory of what went before is gone. Television and other media and statistics pull us back into old realities that may have changed in an instant.

When illusions disappear like the mist before the sun of illumination, a patient unfolding remains in luminous repose.

Thought demands to be pacified by reason. Right action is automatic and requires no thought. Like a stream of pure water it flows unencumbered by reason.

Blame and forgiveness are two sides of one coin. Both are born of blindness to the innocence of all experience.

I exist in boundless oneness.

Many think of accountability as bondage,
but we are accountable first to ourselves
to walk a path of passion and joy.

Joy is the echo of Infinite's Life within us.

The unenlightened oppose others, expecting to
be opposed themselves. The master supports
others in that he knows them to be himself.

Bodily appetites are like an unruly child and must be schooled to know their place, not as needs, but merely as optional desires.

To the caterpillar in the cocoon, his metamorphosis seems catastrophic. The financial system likewise must transfigure.

The incorruptible has always been, yet is ever newly unfolding.

Aloneness yields strength. Aware interaction with others yields warmth. Both are needed for wholeness.

To fear is to abandon the sovereign perfections of the self, creating emptiness within.

The correlation between energy and consciousness demands that you treat your energy as a priceless possession. To squander energy is to disrespect consciousness.

Without wings, stagnation will abound. Without roots,
lack of contented peace will be found. Roots are a
timing mechanism that tempers the speed. Ensuring
the quality of the journey, they fulfill a need.

Transitions can be done with pain or grace.
When oneness is lived, no divisions there
are, thus no transitions take place.

It is not death that kills, but opposition to life. Many say
they do not want to die, but few have ever really lived.

Awakening and sleeping are blended into one.

Nothing can be taken from one part of the ocean and given to another. Like the ocean, life too, will immediately even the score.

Creation wasn't designed for the linear development of individuated life. Linear becoming is an illusion when everything contains all.

The One Life changes all previous possibilities moment by moment. There is absolutely no valid basis for predictability, which is the hallmark of mediocrity.

Beauty, as the true expression of Infinite Life, must renew itself in timelessness. The cosmos does not support the static.

The absolute conviction that the One Life is our unwavering support is our passage to self-sovereignty.

All sub-created realities dissolve to reveal perfection.

The purpose of life is joy. To align with the purpose and spontaneity of life, the inner child must freely express.

Many believe there are key moments we must seize in order to maximize the opportunities of life. Because life is unpredictable, they can only be seen retrospectively and are the unstoppable changes in pace of the One Life.

The changing pace of light happens at the exact right moment – its dance is unstoppable. It is just a privilege for us to participate in turning the keys at critical junctions. But it will change, with or without us.

What is the Dream of life but the unsung notes that slumber as potential in the music?

The real cannot be described, yet it is where perpetual rejuvenation lies.

Authentic expression is not the egoic self's petty desires,
but the becoming of a gateway for the unfathomable.

Nature cannot abide a vacuum, thus what we
fear is attracted in to fill the empty space.

Instead of spending energy on casting blame, winners
spend it in accomplishing. This creates the opportunity
for life to even the score by recompensing you.

The cosmos too has a soul and a spirit. It also goes through life and death experiences. This massive separation can be solved by healing it in a single cell of your body.

Stress is only there when we are in linear time.

Rather than looking at what we cannot do, let us give ourselves credit: it is a supreme act of magic to re-write life.

Neither stillness nor movement is real, but rather stillness in movement and movement in stillness.

The natural unfolding of life is wild and free, rather than 'civilized' and responsible. Having no programs, we follow instead the subtle music flowing from the One Life.

A life of simplicity is not more enlightened than a life of complexity. It just removes the temptation of having our possessions possess us.

Discoveries reveal themselves through
cultivating omni-perspectives.

Power and perception are inseparably connected.
To seek perception, while with false humility
shunning power, is a contradiction.

Through the building blocks of life, the Infinite
illuminates the cosmic unfolding on an endless stage.

Everything we encounter must be approached
as a doorway into the labyrinth of discovery
of the mystery of beingness.

Pain is the language of spirit prompting change.

What is magic but the quickening of events
out of linear progression and linear change?
Magic is where the matrix has no hold.

In the play of life, those who are the planetary light bearers also play the role of life's archetypal pivot points. This subliminal knowledge can urge them to save the world, but life effortlessly pivots through them.

An altered reality obscures the perfection of pristine existence. Pure magic reveals it.

There is nothing for us to align to. Unobstructed by illusory belief systems, life expresses through us.

In not knowing, lies the lightness of life.

If we have fatigue, we have limitations.

Decisions do not exist when Oneness unfolds.
Indecision arises only in the pond that has
been left behind by the ocean's tide.

When we abandon ourselves, the tendency to define ourselves by what we are not becomes strong. Anything that defines itself by its opposite is an illusion.

That which is indivisible cannot
be explained nor denied.

Truth has no opposite and does not exist. Acquired truth is the regurgitated dogma of man.

In a life of no opposites, when the directions come home to the heart and linearity is no more, we become the door of everything.

I am an unfolding work of art.

Wishing to be desired by another is often the mask worn by the need to control.

The body is a dispensable field that can
be replaced by another. It is but a servant.
The real part of us is the master.

If something doesn't go away, it is
because we are not dealing with it.

Like the pressure of the birth canal, life's
illusions increase their pressure at the point
of birthing into a higher consciousness.

The dance of Infinite Life is not one linear flow, but alternating emphasis, unfolding without the need to know.

Because the Infinite speaks through our actions, there can be no freedom of choice. Thus heroism and virtue cannot exist.

Like brilliant feathers through a forest trail, we can but guess at the magnificence of the bird itself.

Healing duality does not mean ending the song by playing all notes at once, but by having each note that is played reflect the whole within it. Let each action be a tribute to the One Life.

The mystical kingdoms are the reflection of the facets of man. As such they do not exist and are as unreal as we are.

Imagination, daydreaming and fantasy are the illusions that replaced nuances. The One Life expresses through alternating nuances.

The body is reshaped by our living in the One Life. The aged may youthen, the care-worn become filled with lightness of being. It is an instrument of delight.

A physical parting cannot occur since the true essence of all beings is like an intermingled field.

When we dwell in separation, the body's false claim to be the self is fed by its demands for attention. When we remember we are one, the body that is unreal dissolves, revealing the incorruptible form of eternal life.

Bodily depletion is an illusion that will vanish
when we see ourselves as living from the place
of no-time where life is always renewed.

The perfection of life cannot be tarnished.
There is nothing but self-regulating wholeness.
The eons of seeming illusion are nothing but
the oyster that opens to reveal the pearl.

Individuation comes from the shadows that surround
that which is illuminated by the One Life.

The Dance of the One Life is not an undisciplined
life; it moves through us and helps us become
a master artist versus a clumsy participant.

As unique expressions of the Infinite, eternal yet
ever new, our bodies are sacred. Let us honor these
instruments of grace as living temples of divinity.

Separation causes self-reflection and comparison.
These in turn cause self-pity or self-importance.
In recognizing oneness, the beauty and
admirable qualities of all become ours.

Abundance in Expression

The moment is an illusion that promises to eliminate linear time, but instead causes it. Life in no-time sets us free from the tyranny of form and space.

Suffering is not the tool of discipline, nor the test of worthiness. It is the result of opposition to life.

All light bodies or higher aspects of ourselves have been consolidated into the physical. Our guidance comes directly from the Infinite's Intent.

By imagining ourselves as being the mind, the emotions and the body, we believe that loss can be a reality; like a child crying for its mother who is in another room. By knowing ourselves as the eternal vastness containing all, separation cannot occur.

The symbols of our dreams point out where life can be lived more authentically and with more joyous discovery.

Our wholeness cannot be tainted when we live life from the perfection of Beingness. The illusory life of form is then a malleable tool to the One Life

He who knows himself to be the All is
wealthy indeed, for he is heir to the starry
skies and the silk of a spider's web alike.

The dance of light and shadow through space must
yield its illusory beauty for the conjunction of
expressions of Infinite Oneness – true beauty.

Impressions cannot be lasting within the One Life where
everything changes from moment to moment. This allows
life to change with it rather than hold onto the old.

Because there is but One Being in existence, the
momentary gap that seems to appear when giving
to another is immediately being filled by life.

Creation will always be a base illusion. It
cannot exist as a separate space, but rather as
the unfolding nuances of the Infinite.

Do not accept poverty as being virtuous.
The very nature of life is abundance.

Life is a perfectly directed play and every being plays his part. Even if there is seeming apathy on the part of a character, it is written into the script.

When we live from the fullness of Infinite Presence, only the illusion that supports the dance remains. That which trips the grace of the dancer dissolves.

All levels of consciousness are equal in their contribution to the One. The same perfection flows through the sage and the fool.

The contraction of vision that focused on the
details and produced duality has been changed.
Humanity is able to see all perspectives at once.

Let us move with loving attention and full surrender
to the ever-changing nuances of the One Life.

Innocence can be cruel because its self-centeredness
can't understand another's pain. Purity opens
its heart in compassionate understanding.

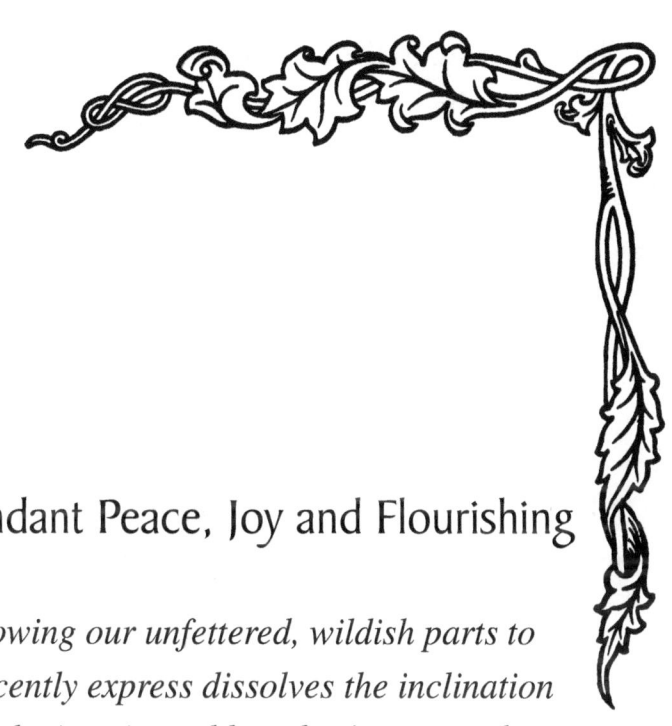

Abundant Peace, Joy and Flourishing

*Allowing our unfettered, wildish parts to
innocently express dissolves the inclination
to be imprisoned by other's approval
and trapped by social expectations.*

Surrendering to the solitariness of finding there is no being other than Ourselves, transitions us to the eventual fullness of knowing Ourselves to be all things.

Where the One Life is seen, desires flee. What is there to need when all is within? What hunger can there be when all is obtained and there is nothing to feed?

Incorruptibility dances with the paradox of illusion, embracing the unknowable essence of life and begins to draw from the endless supply of the One Life. But there is a stage beyond the paradox of formless form and spaceless space – Absolute Oneness. It is then that we become the paradox.

Let life unfold through us spontaneously and
guilelessly, cradled in the knowledge that
life is benevolent to all individuations.

Life is the song of the Infinite and each
person you meet is one of its notes.

When Oneness creates a life of no opposites,
equilibrium is the nature of reality. From the
soil of equilibrium, flowering occurs.

The Infinite Life does not have desired outcomes, but rather spontaneously expresses. Blended with the One, we dance along to the music.

Disconnecting from the group consciousness of humanity requires unfailing trust that beyond the appearances of decay lies a timeless perfection.

The dissolving of the illusion that form is real will allow us to experience life directly as it is.

It is in simplicity that the true riches of life are found. It can then be said that poverty is the new abundance.

When memory is dissolved and effortless knowing takes its place, the new expression of life gracefully eliminates what is not pertinent to the moment.

The disciplined master does not treat the past as real by looking back. Time does not exist. All knowledge reveals itself when we stay in the moment within silence of the mind. This is effortless knowing.

There is neither youth nor age – just the response
of our eternal fluid form to our belief systems.

There is no point of origin or arrival. There
is no need for haste or striving when life
is seen from the eternal perspective.

All successful achievers know that they write
the script of the play of their lives. As they see
themselves as abundant, so they become.

In the silent depths of your being, concepts
like power, movement and growth fall
away, yielding to rapturous peace.

The language of instinct speaks through the
spontaneous expression of living art, setting
us free from the chains of the intellect.

Light-seekers diligently weed the garden of the soul, but
often forget to sow the seeds of contentment and delight.

The soul as the formless, like the body as the formed, is still but an illusion. Individuation cannot exist within the One.

Watch carefully the ripples of irritation in the river of your life. They are not a hindrance, but a help. Beneath the ripples lie the prevalent insights required to further your growth.

Living in no-time does not mean that you do not pay attention to what is before you, but that what is before you is all that is.

No potential can exist in the one who dwells
beyond opposites. All is fully lived in Oneness.

The burden of being the pivot point for the
growth of the cosmos has been removed from
the few and re-distributed to the many. Wherever
authentic living takes place, life flourishes.

In seeking to eliminate our flaws, life becomes
depleted unless the gaps they leave are filled. It is in
the laughter of the heart that seeds of potential grow.

Through trusting surrender, the grand adventure of
my existence inspires me into fuller expression.

Contentment arises from the knowledge that
wherever we are in the moment has taken eons
to achieve and is therefore our greatest gift.

Those who flourish in hard financial times
are those who find creative solutions, rather
than focusing on the problems.

Life has no opposites. It is only in opposing
life that we create the illusion that opposites
exist. This creates the illusion of death.

Only by living from all the depths of our being
can we express unlimited excellence.

Whether you choose to see life's chaos or Oneness,
you need not engage it – only envelop it.

The play of life changes depending on
what you obscure from yourself. If you do
not like the play, gain the insights.

Celebrate success but do not take it seriously.
Neither success nor failure can be ours when
there is only One Life expressing.

Redefine abundance as having all you need
and not needing all you have. Most mistakenly
regard extravagant excess as abundance.

When certain resources are emphasized in an
individual's life, others are de-emphasized.
Discover with gratitude where your wealth lies.

Hold lightly to the joy of the moment
lest you fade with it into the past.

In pouring our love into what we do,
excellence is born to gild the moment and
shed light on the path of existence.

If tomorrow is forged by this moment, but
this moment is spent living in the future,
where will tomorrow come from?

Beauty that reflects the unobstructed expression
of the One Life cannot change or fade.

When deep elation fills your soul, you
have just lived your highest truth.

Fluidity is the key factor to success in financially trying times. Consider temporary options and multiple jobs.

There are those who look back and exclaim, "If only." There are those who look forward and say, "Next time." Then there are those who masterfully enjoy what the moment brings.

In seeing our work as a means to an end, our labor yields mediocrity.

Whatever you manifested before, your being
is capable of doing the same or better again.
Live with hope and without regrets.

Death and birth can never be too late or too
early. The scale only tips when one side reaches
the exact measure that makes it heavier.

Through the Oneness of All, life metamorphoses
into a higher expression of divinity.

When life is a living work of art, the whisperings of source express through all we do. Art bypasses the conscious and sub-conscious minds as a non-cognitive communication from the Infinite.

Life seems to be the One expressing as the many. Rather, it is the many expressing as the One. In your reality, you are all that is; relationships therefore do not exist.

Do not fear adversity. What is a symphony without its low notes? When the storm winds blow through the seasons of your life, the loving embrace of the Infinite will shelter you.

Fulfillment begins by rejoicing in what you have.
Change begins in accepting where you are. Increase
begins in being grateful for your supply.

The attitude of praise can become a deep spiritual
practice until every cell eventually sings its song.
This is truly the power and glory of praise.

What we perceive as obstacles, life
turns into symbols of inclusion.

Fear exists that when we experience the vastness, we may dissociate from life. The life we detach from is not real life; we detach from the unreal without separation.

The sub-creations of our man-made world cannot exist. The real cannot be created by the unreal.

The only freedom that exists is the freedom from thinking that anything can be bound by the unreal.

Personalities form so that we do not
get taken back into Oneness.

Obstacles are but the illusory guidelines that direct
the steps of the dance of life. We can also use the
more pleasant method of following our joy.

To live from the abundant depths of our being is
to leave mind behind. Mind ties us to its shallow
creation – personality. Instinctual knowing assesses
the ever-unfolding nature of our being.

In our fellow man and all around us, the praiseworthy lies like the gems of dewdrops on a spider web, waiting to be discovered.

Remember, a challenge is merely a piece of the mystery of being that we have, as yet, not solved.

All comfort zones consist of the familiar and the known, whether one is in ego-identification or the mastery of expansion. Life must become the unknowable to become one with the Infinite.

The body expressing in spaceless space is a fluid part of the dance, no longer a rigid reference point in the boundlessness of our being.

Life-affirming and joyous innovation is the true reality of life. To try and steer its course is as futile as trying to harness the clouds.

The strength of the bear, the speed of the rabbit, the freedom of an eagle's flight – all live within us, awaiting expression. The One Life has no room for personality, but instead, the fullness of existence is ours.

Living vibrantly gives others permission to do so also. It furthermore creates a resonance within them that awakens their own vibrancy.

Beauty can only be seen when the mind is still and the heart is open. What is beauty but the momentary glimpse of Eternity.

No external approval is needed, for we have been created for the sake of delight. There is nothing to accomplish other than deep enjoyment of life.

Let your heart's guidance be the sovereign dictator
of your life. It is the seat of your highest wisdom
and the wellspring of the creativity of your life.

Through us the One Life expresses flawlessly and in
spite of ourselves. The gentle violin and the thunderous
drums have equally important parts in the symphony.

Artistic expression is life revealed. True art,
like glimpsing a nuance of the Infinite's face,
leaves us with a refined appreciation of life.

When you wipe the fog from your
eyes, you will see the real.

Rejuvenation requires inner power to transcend the matrix of cycles of life and death. Power is the result of increased perception – seeing what we have never conceived of before. Overcoming aging and decay thus requires seeing beyond the horizons of mortal boundaries.

The seeming happiness of those living on the treadmill of life is an illusion. Happiness is not fulfillment of our desires, but fulfillment without having desires.

Abundance comes from healing the duality of life
by seeing the divine order behind appearances
– knowing that the Infinite sends nothing but
good. There may be gifts or lessons, but the
latter is just an elaborate disguise for gifts.

There is no destiny or fate. No divine mission we need to
fulfill awaits us. It is the tyranny of reason that demands
we justify our existence beyond the joy of living.

Laugh every day so resources can flow. Be
silly and funny, as a child would play.

Slow momentum and all flows by you. When you strive for results, the river of supply flows the opposite way.

The tendency to label parts of life in order to pacify reason and provide the illusion of predictability enslaves us to form. To circumvent this, we experience life with complete attention to the moment, freely acknowledging that because everything is renewed in every moment, we can know nothing.

Genius has no intellect. It is present in the master who has achieved emptiness of mind through complete surrender, as effortless knowing.

We are not shaped by past experiences, for
time does not exist. We are as new as the
moment, yet ageless without beginning.

The belief that only one form can occupy one
space at a time is unreal. Since form is an illusion,
man should be able to walk through walls.

Being open to receiving, as well as giving, is to know
that we are a player on the stage of life and that in
performing either role, we honor the value of the play.

As life moves through us, its dance can be performed
with enjoyment or resistance. Enjoyment comes
from the contentment that results from surrender.

Humor is the experience of entering into the rapture
of the movement of the One Life. Laughter is
the release of such a momentous experience.

The measure of a person is not how far down he has
been, but how much he has overcome. Do not look
back or you may define yourself by what you have
been, rather than by what you are becoming.

What is love but the yearning for the divinity within as it is briefly reflected in the eyes of another? Like an elusive butterfly that beckons with its splendor, it tempts us to reach without for that which slumbers within.

Embrace the magic of your physical world and the heat of your passions, that total balance may come into your life.

As the beauty of the Earth yields to your awareness, you claim it as your own. Life thrives on appreciation and abundance comes from awareness.

When we live like a child, experiencing without
mind life's bounteous endless flow, life will provide
all we desire – then true abundance we will know.

Life is a dance of tranquility and revelry,
filled with the merry madness of delight.

Understanding life is not possible if we realize that
there is no preconceived plan of expression, but rather
a spontaneous display of the Infinite's self-enjoyment.

As we embrace more and more of life we become one with other creatures, assembling their realities within us as well. The will of the Embodiment of the Infinite blends with ours more and more.

Bringing gifts of joy to another is nothing more than becoming an open channel for life flowing through itself.

It is in quietness and surrendered contentment that we access the true wealth of our being – the perfection lying like diamonds in the dust of belief systems.

The dissolving of an illusion releases its resources like a fragrance that revivifies and enchants all life.

Let friendship be for inspiration and delight, whether for a moment or eternity. We are a traveler on life's journey and in our unfolding, never the same.

To use hormone replacement therapy is to lock us into mortality and decay. Hormones are the messengers of the body and as consciousness rises, hormonal messages change. Stimulating our own natural production is the answer.

All that has had a beginning within the Eternal Being, such as mind or intelligence, is an illusion.

Neither expansion nor contraction can exist. There is just inseparable Oneness of Life, experiencing without perspective the unfolding of Its Being.

The fear of annihilation has arisen as a result of the ending of cycles. However, the real part of all of us is without beginning or end.

In the absence of mind and emotions,
I live an existence of rapture.

Let us create works of art of every moment.
Let our whole life be lived from the perspective
of the poetic and as a living work of art.

Embracing truth as an eternal presence
acknowledges that it cannot be a static concept,
but rather an ever-changing flow.

Surrender is not the loss of freedom. It is freedom.

All is in full expression through the smallest feather of a bird. The form reveals but a fragment of what lies at the heart of form.

By acknowledging the reality we live in to be unreal, exiting the matrix can be accomplished. Life can be miraculous when orchestrated from the timeless reality of the One Life.

This moment well-lived changes past
karma; in fact, it changes the past.

Form is a doorway into Infinity – each
doorway revealing to eyes that can see,
an emphasized quality of the whole.

Age is like a dream that never really happened. Because
age does not really exist, neither does rejuvenation.
In realizing this, illusory signs of aging disappear.

The more we know ourselves as the only
being in existence, the more we are able
to impact the quality of the Dream.

No accomplishment can be repeated, for no two
moments are the same. Even greater accomplishments
await the one whose inspiration is the Endless Source.

We have no freedom of choice in that our choices
are those of the One Life. How we produce
quality in those choices – that is our choice.

Find the greater life by letting the lesser go.

To prepare for the worst in order to have the luxury of expecting the best, was a sound philosophy when growth came through opposition. In this new paradigm, where growth comes through support, it is an act of faithlessness.

Nothing is created – just seen anew. In different levels of luminosity, depending on how many pretended veils of illusion there are, it shines through.

In treating money as crystallized power, with intention, empower what you spend money on. Taxes create amenities that better society – envision that.

Forsaking all belief systems, authenticity remains.

To truly experience another is a matter of the heart. The mind and senses can only appreciate the form, but the heart can know the divine essence within.

In self-acknowledged divinity, our footsteps
bless the Earth that all life may flourish.

The spontaneous Song of the One Life is directed by
inspiration found in the most unlikely of places. It is
often the gap between notes that speaks most eloquently.

One may see confinements and thus feel victimized.
Another finds a wonderland in the light of another's eyes.

Karma is the shadow cast by not seeing things within.

With greed in their hearts, some clutch at the fleeting riches of life like a beggar craving alms. The crumbs of existence come to the one who cannot see the unfathomable wealth within. To he who is in Oneness, all needs dissolve.

Creativity is the essence of unfolding life. If we do not have creativity as part of our lives, we also do not have access to its resources.

Let recovery from financial setbacks become a family affair that children may learn how to cheerfully and optimistically adjust to life's vicissitudes.

Our societies have generated enslavement to work and class-based structures. These illusions have become tyrants.

Many do not seek out the healing pristineness of nature, fearing they may be bored. But it is not boredom they fear, but silence. It is in the silences of our lives that we encounter ourselves.

The greatest gifts we give to life are the overcomings
of duality within. Through this all are uplifted.

Don't look back at life's crests and valleys
of waves that no longer exist, but surf with
cooperation, the wave that forms in the moment.

When beauty is seen with the heart, we
connect the real part of ourselves to the real
part of life. We enter into the One Life.

All perception is really self-perception because you can only recognize that which is within you.

To allow others to affect the quality of your day is to navigate your life like a rudderless ship, subject to being tossed about by the shifting breezes.

In living from your highest identity as a consciousness superimposed over all that is, the cosmos becomes your resource library. Breathe in the timelessness of the stars, the newness of the dawn, the fluid grace of the river.

We create reality by affirming it through inner and outer dialogue. The dialogue of the mind affirms reality.

There are those who are patient and those
who are impatient. Then there are those who,
living beyond the existence of opposites,
simply delight in unfolding timelessness.

Our little selves have no freedom of choice.
All of life is directed by the One Life. The only
way to be free is to become the One Life.

Weave your dreams and hopes into reality
from the river of the starry skies that flows
through the endlessness of your being.

Ask in the awake-time whether you are awake
or asleep, know that when separation abounds,
you are in a dream within a dream.

Tomorrow is a variable waiting to be written. The past is like a wave, that for a fleeting moment, graced the shore. This moment is the gateway to the wealth of eternity.

Do not wait for others to do what you can do for yourself. Be courageous and step up; make yourself strong and do what is your responsibility to do.

Through integrated Oneness, healing comes.

We schedule the activities of our busy life - why do we not schedule with equal commitment the solitude that feeds the depth of our lives and reveals the whispering inspiration of our being?

A life of grace produces refined awareness in
your children. It is not the result of haphazard
chaos but the culmination of a disciplined
life lived with artistry and elegance.

The present is a fluidly eternal moment.

We live as the ocean of the unknown, always
renewing our Self-expression. All around us is
always new and needs to be explored by us.

The concept of permanence, arising from the divisions created by mind, is in opposition to the ever-new unfolding of life. Immortal incorruptibility is the becoming of life's fluid expression.

All of our being becomes self-sustaining when joy opens the gates of indivisible Oneness. No dependency can exist when we know our self-sustenance.

When we are all beings, there is only One Life. Relationship cannot have an actual existence. It is a role we play within ourselves.

No need to see outcome for hope to abound, not when trusting surrender in the One Life is found.

Life is no longer a process of seeking to become.
It is instead a flowering of where we are.

Wherever life exists, there perfection is also.

Our individuation is a delight to the Infinite
One Life or else we would not exist at
all. Delight is the purpose of life.

To live a life of awareness is to see and
value what is life-enhancing.

Trusting in the benevolence of life allows us to
experience the moment with the innocence of a
child, unconcerned with tomorrow's supply.

Bless your walls of illusions for the comfort they have brought to let you unfold at your own pace.

There can only be courage when we see life as adverse. In full and complete trust in life's benevolence, there is only surrender.

We are fulfilling our destiny, whether we know it or not.

The prerequisite to achieving the rapture
of surrender into Oneness is trust through
releasing all resistance created by mind.

There is no set of plans for our lives, hence no
destiny to unfold. Life's script has not yet been
written – it is spontaneously produced.

He who enjoys the discovery of life
opens the doors of heaven within.

Release the addiction to the tension of physicality through surrender; becoming a wave that melts into the ocean.

The joy of what is there now, opens up the possibilities of the future. Joy is the desire to keep what it appreciates. Happiness is the continual inspiration joyous moments bring.

The matrices of reality that we fight against are nothing but the veils with which the Infinite slowly reveals Its face.

Let's live a life of inspiration! Not one from expectation.

Excellence does not lie in the end product,
but in the expression that produces it.

Treating each day as though it represents forever,
consciously creates wealth of living.

In the clarity of an illusion-less life,
let us celebrate beingness.

Life spins on a dime, and if we enter the next moment without expectation, the ability to salvage the day may yet present itself.

Magnificent and accelerated changes occur in the cosmos every day. Fluidity, as the hallmark of mastery, acknowledges this.

In the lonely pine tree, rooted in the rocky heights of inhospitable cliffs and embattled by winds, we see the indomitable and unconquerable fortitude of the human spirit.

Self-trust knows that we are guided to make the right decision as long as we live our heart's truth, purely and without agenda. We then know there are really no failures, only growth.

Closing

Q. *What is the value of wisdom, when the more I seek it, the less I know?*
A. The worth of wisdom is that the seeker discovers that around in a circle he goes. The greatest gift that wisdom can give is its own illusions to show.

Q. *What lies beyond wisdom that I can seek and ultimately hope to find?*
A. The ending of wisdom is the beginning of the contradiction of life.

Q. *I hear it shine through wisdom's words, yet no description of the One Life have I heard.*
A. That which is real cannot be described, for it lies beyond the confines of understanding.

Q. *Then how shall I know the Infinite's voice?*
A. The song of the Infinite is all there is. To interpret it, you have no choice. Thus, seek not to understand the glorious paradox of life, for no creation can. Cease to strive, and dance with delight to the song of eternal life.

Related products created by Almine

Irash Satva Yoga
The Yoga of Abundance

Yoga, as a spiritual and physical discipline has been practiced in many variations by masters and novices for countless years and is universally accepted as one of the most effective development tools ever created.

Man's physical form in its original state was meant to be self-purifying, self-regenerating and self-transfiguring. Through pristine living and total surrender, it was possible to open gates in the body that would allow life to permeate and flow through it; indefinitely sustaining it.

In Irash Satva Yoga, received by Almine from the Angelic Kingdom, this ancient methodology is exponentially expanded and enhanced by incorporating the alchemies of sound and frequency.

Using easily mastered postures paired with music from Cosmic Sources created specifically for each, the 144 cardinal gates in the mind and body are opened and cleansed of their dross and debris, allowing the practitioner to tap into the abundance of the One Life.

Published: 2010, 94 pages, soft cover, 6 x 9, $24.95, ISBN: 978-1-934070-95-6

Shrihat Satva Yoga
The Yoga to Clear Past Incarnations

The human body is unique in that it is an exact microcosm of the macrocosm of created life. There are 12 points along the right, masculine side of the body and the same number on the left side. These are microcosmic replicas of the macrocosmic cycles of life.

The yoga postures are designed to open and remove the debris from these points — the gates of dreaming. This will occur physically through the postures and the music. Dissolving debris also occurs by way of dreaming (triggered by the breathing and eye movements), releasing past issues that caused the blockages in the points

Published 2010, 108 pages, soft cover, 6 x 9, $34.95, ISBN: 978-1-934070-15-4

Saradesi Satva Yoga
The Yoga of Eternal Youth
As translated from the ancient texts of Saradesi – The Fountain of Youth. The ancient texts speak of time as movement. They affirm that time and space, movement and stillness, are illusions. To sustain any illusion requires an enormous amount of resources. This depletion of resources causes aging and decay. The illusion of polarity, the impossibility that the One Life can be divided and split is brought to resolution by balancing the opposite poles exactly. Only then can they cancel one another out, revealing an incorruptible reality that lies beyond – the reality of Eternal Youth.

Published 2011, 115 pages, soft cover, 6 x 9, $24.95, ISBN: 978-1-936926-05-3

Secrets of Rejuvenation
Discovering the Fountain of Youth
Rejuvenation through physical methods alone creates an inner conflict resulting in inflammatory physical conditions.

Opposition arises from limiting belief systems and worldviews that obstruct open channels of the limitless resources available from Source.

From the ancient records of Saradesi come paradigm transcending philosophies, coupled with physical practices to enhance the body's natural inclination to rejuvenate. Almine has proven it is possible to rejuvenate. Here are the secrets.

Published: 2010, 219 pages, soft cover, 6 x 9, $19.95, ISBN: 978-1-934070-52-9

How to Raise an Exceptional Child
Practical Wisdom for Spiritual Mastery
Safeguarding the purity of our children in a world of escalating materialism, requires a deep understanding and wisdom on the part of the parents, grandparents and other caregivers.

They walk among us seemingly as ordinary children. But then we look again, for something in their eyes catches our attention – a certain knowingness, an ancient wisdom coupled with a purity so profound that it stops us in our tracks. Surely the masters throughout the ages, the light-bearers of humanity, looked out at the world with just such clarity.

Published: 2010, 215 pages, soft cover, 6 x 9, $19.95, ISBN: 978-1-9349979-11-2

Visit Almine's website www.spiritualjourneys.com for worldwide retreat locations and dates, online courses, radio shows and more. Order one of Almine's many books, CDs or an instant download.
US toll-free phone 1-877-552-5646

Music by Almine

Children of the Sun
Music from the Known Planets (Re-mastered and re-titled version of the Interstellar Sound Elixirs)
The beautiful interstellar sound elixirs received and sung by Almine.

Price $9.95 MP3 Download
$14.95 CD

Labyrinth of the Moon
Music from the Hidden Planets (Re-titled version of the Sound Elixirs of the Hidden Planets)
All the vocals in these elixirs are received and sung in the moment by Almine

Price $9.95 MP3 Download
$14.95 CD

Jubilation - Songs of Praise
Music from around the world to lift the heart and inspire the listener.
The extraordinary mystical quality of the music, and the exquisite clarity of Almine's voice, creates the ambient impression of being in the presence of angels.

Price $9.95 MP3 Download
$14.95 CD

www.ingramcontent.com/pod-product-compliance
Lightning Source LLC
Chambersburg PA
CBHW060448170426
43199CB00011B/1133